THRESHOLD BIBLE STUDY

THE CHURCH'S PRAYERS AT DUSK

Psalms of the Evening

STEPHEN J. BINZ

TWENTY-THIRD PUBLICATIONS
twentythirdpublications.com

TWENTY-THIRD PUBLICATIONS
977 Hartford Turnpike Unit A
Waterford, CT 06385
(860) 437-3012 or (800) 321-0411
www.twentythirdpublications.com

Images: stock.adobe.com

ISBN: 978-1-62785-825-0
Printed in the U.S.A.

What People Are Saying about *Threshold Bible Study*

"Falling in love with the sacred scriptures enables us to fall in deeper love with our loving God. *Threshold Bible Study* helps us see the Word of God alive in us and among us."

Archbishop Gregory M. Aymond, *Archbishop of New Orleans*

"The books in Stephen Binz's *Threshold Bible Study* read like *lectio divina* meditations from the monastic tradition, but with fascinating historical insights about the biblical characters and authors. He has a gift for making these ancient texts speak an urgent but compelling word to us today, inviting us to read ourselves into the great drama of salvation history. He nourishes the roots of our Christian faith in the rich soil of Judaism, and he presents the Bible as a single fountain with an endlessly fresh supply of water for anyone thirsting for the Lord."

Thomas Esposito, O. Cist., *Professor of Theology, University of Dallas*

"*Threshold Bible Study* enables Catholics to read, with greater understanding, the Bible in the Church."

Francis Cardinal George, OMI, *the late Archbishop Emeritus of Chicago*

"The Church has called Scripture a 'font' and 'wellspring' for the spiritual life. *Threshold Bible Study* is one of the best sources for tapping into the biblical font. *Threshold Bible Study* offers you an encounter with the word that will make your heart come alive."

Tim Gray, *President of the Augustine Institute, Denver*

"Stephen Binz's *Threshold Bible Study* expertly blends deep scholarly insight with warm, approachable language, perfectly suiting both group and individual study. Binz's engaging style makes profound spiritual truths accessible and relatable, offering a transformative experience for those seeking to deepen their faith through an encounter with sacred Scripture. This series is a treasure for anyone looking to explore the Bible in a fresh and life-changing way. It serves as a beautiful gateway of grace for those yearning to enrich their faith journey."

Kris McGregor, *founder and director of DiscerningHearts.com and host of* ***Inside the Pages***

"Inviting, accessible, and wise, *Threshold Bible Study* is an absolutely superb resource for all Catholics interested in unlocking the Living Word. You now have no excuse not to read and enjoy the Bible."

James Martin, SJ, *Editor-at-large at America media, author of* ***Jesus: A Pilgrimage***

"*Threshold Bible Study* guides readers to 'do justice, love kindness, and walk humbly with God,' reflecting on Scripture and acting on its prophetic call. Stephen Binz uses his biblical scholarship and passion for God's word to show others how to take on the mind and heart of Jesus through a meditative reading of Scripture. I recommend this approach to Bible study because it spotlights key themes of biblical revelation and underscores their contemporary importance."

■ **Helen Prejean, CSJ**, *Activist in opposition to the death penalty, author of* ***Dead Man Walking*** *and* ***River of Fire****, New Orleans*

"Stephen J. Binz is a consistently outstanding Catholic educator and communicator whose books on the study and application of Scripture have thoroughly enriched my Christian understanding. In our fast-moving, often confusing times, his ability to help us examine and comprehend the truth through all the noise is especially needed and valuable."

■ **Elizabeth Scalia**, *writer and blogger as The Anchoress*

"Stephen Binz has created an essential resource for the new evangelization rooted in the discipleship process that helps participants to unpack the treasures of the Scriptures in an engaging and accessible manner. *Threshold Bible Study* connects faith learning to faithful living, leading one to a deeper relationship with Christ and his body, the Church."

■ **Julianne Stanz**, *Director of New Evangelization, Diocese of Green Bay*

"*Threshold Bible Study* provides a very engaging approach and encounter with sacred Scripture, all the while encouraging the faithful to listen and discern the Word of God, especially in and through Jesus Christ."

■ **Archbishop Charles C. Thompson**, *Archbishop of Indianapolis*

"*Threshold Bible Study* draws readers into an experience of the word of God through intricately researched historical details along with a profound spirituality of the Scriptures. Encountering Christ through the Word provides light for our lives, hope for our hearts, and passion to share this word with everyone. Thanks to Stephen Binz's scholarship, readers can delve deeply into God's love letter to humanity."

■ **Nancy Usselmann, FSP**, *Director of Pauline Center for Media Studies*

"*Threshold Bible Study* is a wonderful publication that is sure to open new doors for every reader. In a practical, pastoral, and accessible manner, Stephen Binz brings the insights of contemporary scholarship to us in understandable language and clear format, inviting readers to deeper reflection on their own lived experience."

■ **Bishop Kevin Vann**, *Bishop of Orange, California*

Contents

LESSONS 13–18

LESSONS 19–24

LESSONS 25–30

How to Use *Threshold Bible Study*

Threshold Bible Study is a dynamic, informative, inspiring, and life-changing series that helps you learn about Scripture in a whole new way. Each book will help you explore new dimensions of faith and discover deeper insights for your life as a disciple of Jesus.

The threshold is a place of transition. The threshold of God's word invites you to enter that place where God's truth, goodness, and beauty can shine into your life and fill your mind and heart. Through the Holy Spirit, the threshold becomes holy ground, sacred space, and graced time. God can teach you best at the threshold, because God opens your life to his word and fills you with the Spirit of truth.

With *Threshold Bible Study,* each topic or book of the Bible is approached in a thematic way. You will understand and reflect on the biblical texts through overarching themes derived from biblical theology. Through this method, the study of Scripture will impact your life in a unique way and transform you from within.

These books are designed for maximum flexibility. Each study is presented in a workbook format, with sections for reading, reflecting, writing, discussing, and praying. Each *Threshold* book contains thirty lessons, which you can use for your daily study over the course of a month or which can be divided into six lessons per week, providing a group study of six weekly sessions. These studies are ideal for Bible study groups, small Christian communities, adult faith formation, student groups, Sunday school, neighborhood groups, and family reading, as well as for individual learning.

The commentary that follows each biblical passage launches your reflection on that passage and helps you begin to see its significance within the context of your contemporary experience. The questions following the commentary challenge you to understand the passage more fully and apply it to your own life. Space for writing after each question is ideal for personal study and also allows group participants to prepare for the weekly discussion. The prayer helps conclude your study each day by integrating your learning into your relationship with God.

The method of *Threshold Bible Study* is rooted in the ancient tradition of *lectio divina,* whereby studying the Bible becomes a means of deeper intimacy with God and a transformed life. Reading and interpreting the text (*lectio*) is followed by reflective meditation on its message (*meditatio*). This reading and reflecting flows into prayer from the heart (*oratio* and *contemplatio*). In this way, one listens to God through the Scripture and then responds to God in prayer.

This ancient method assures you that Bible study is a matter of both the mind and the heart. It is not just an intellectual exercise to learn more and be able to discuss the Bible with others. It is, more importantly, a transforming experience. Reflecting on God's word, guided by the Holy Spirit, illumines the mind with wisdom and stirs the heart with zeal.

Following the personal Bible study, *Threshold Bible Study* offers ways to extend personal *lectio divina* into a weekly conversation with others. This communal experience will allow participants to enhance their appreciation of the message and build up a spiritual community (*collatio*). The end result will be to increase not only individual faith but also faithful witness in the context of daily life (*operatio*).

When bringing *Threshold Bible Study* to a church community, try to make every effort to include as many people as possible. Many will want to study on their own; others will want to study with family, a group of friends, or a few work associates; some may want to commit themselves to share insights through a weekly conference call, daily text messaging, or an online social network; and others will want to gather weekly in established small groups.

By encouraging *Threshold Bible Study* and respecting the many ways people desire to make Bible study a regular part of their lives, you will widen the number of people in your church community who study the Bible regularly in whatever way they are able in their busy lives. Simply sign up people at the Sunday services and order bulk quantities for your church. Encourage people to follow the daily study as faithfully as they can. This encouragement can be through Sunday announcements, notices in parish publications, support on the church website, and other creative invitations and motivations.

Through the spiritual disciplines of Scripture reading, study, reflection, conversation, and prayer, *Threshold Bible Study* will help you experience God's grace more abundantly and root your life more deeply in Christ. The risen Jesus said: "Listen! I am standing at the door, knocking; if you hear my voice and open the door, I will come in to you and eat with you, and you with me" (Rev 3:20). Listen to the word of God, open the door, and cross the threshold to an unimaginable dwelling with God!

SUGGESTIONS FOR INDIVIDUAL STUDY

- Make your Bible reading a time of prayer. Ask for God's guidance as you read the Scriptures.
- Try to study daily, or as often as possible according to the circumstances of your life.
- Read the Bible passage carefully, trying to understand both its meaning and its personal application as you read. Some persons find it helpful to read the passage aloud.
- Read the passage in another Bible translation. Each version adds to your understanding of the original text.
- Allow the commentary to help you comprehend and apply the scriptural text. The commentary is only a beginning, not the last word, on the meaning of the passage.
- After reflecting on each question, write out your responses. The very act of writing will help you clarify your thoughts, bring new insights, and amplify your understanding.
- As you reflect on your answers, think about how you can live God's word in the context of your daily life.
- Conclude each daily lesson by reading the prayer and continuing with your own prayer from the heart.
- Make sure your reflections and prayers are matters of both the mind and the heart. A true encounter with God's word is always a transforming experience.
- Choose a word or a phrase from the lesson to carry with you throughout the day as a reminder of your encounter with God's life-changing word.
- For additional insights and affirmation, share your learning experience with at least one other person whom you trust. The ideal way to share learning is in a small group that meets regularly.

SUGGESTIONS FOR GROUP STUDY

- Meet regularly; weekly is ideal. Try to be on time and make attendance a high priority for the sake of the group. The average group meets for about an hour.
- Open each session with a prepared prayer, a song, or a reflection. Find some appropriate way to bring the group from the workaday world into a sacred time of graced sharing.
- If you have not been together before, name tags are very helpful as a group begins to become acquainted with the other group members.
- Spend the first session getting acquainted with one another, reading the Introduction aloud, and discussing the questions that follow.
- Appoint a group facilitator to provide guidance to the discussion. The role of facilitator may rotate among members each week. The facilitator simply keeps the discussion on track; each person shares responsibility for the group. There is no need for the facilitator to be a trained teacher.
- Try to study the six lessons on your own during the week. When you have done your own reflection and written your own answers, you will be better prepared to discuss the six scriptural lessons with the group. If you have not had an opportunity to study the passages during the week, meet with the group anyway to share support and insights.
- Participate in the discussion as much as you are able, offering your thoughts, insights, feelings, and decisions. You learn by sharing with others the fruits of your study.
- Be careful not to dominate the discussion. It is important that everyone in the group be offered an equal opportunity to share the results of their work. Try to link what you say to the comments of others so that the group remains on the topic.
- When discussing your own personal thoughts or feelings, use "I" language. Be as personal and honest as appropriate and be very cautious about giving advice to others.

- Listen attentively to the other members of the group so as to learn from their insights. The words of the Bible affect each person in a different way, so a group provides a wealth of understanding for each member.
- Don't fear silence. Silence in a group is as important as silence in personal study. It allows individuals time to listen to the voice of God's Spirit and the opportunity to form their thoughts before they speak.
- Solicit several responses for each question. The thoughts of different people will build on the answers of others and will lead to deeper insights for all.
- Don't fear controversy. Differences of opinions are a sign of a healthy and honest group. If you cannot resolve an issue, continue on, agreeing to disagree. There is probably some truth in each viewpoint.
- Discuss the questions that seem most important for the group. There is no need to cover all the questions in the group session.
- Realize that some questions about the Bible cannot be resolved, even by experts. Don't get stuck on some issue for which there are no clear answers.
- Whatever is said in the group is said in confidence and should be regarded as such.
- Pray as a group in whatever way feels comfortable. Pray for the members of your group throughout the week.

Schedule for Group Study

Session 1: Introduction Date: ______________________

Session 2: Lessons 1–6 Date: ______________________

Session 3: Lessons 7–12 Date: ______________________

Session 4: Lessons 13–18 Date: ______________________

Session 5: Lessons 19–24 Date: ______________________

Session 6: Lessons 25–30 Date: ______________________

THE PSALMS
DAY 4. EVENING PRAYER
PSALM 22. Deus, Deus meus

Let my prayer be counted as incense before you, and the lifting up of my hands as an evening sacrifice. Set a guard over my mouth, O Lord; keep watch over the door of my lips. PSALM 141:2–3

The Church's Prayers at Dusk

The triumphant splendor of sunset is a favorable time to review our day before God in prayer, a time to give thanks for the blessings of the day and to express our trust in God as the shadows lengthen and the light gives way to the darkness of night. Evening is also the time for the lighting of oil lamps and candles, both a practical and expressive gesture of care and protection. In religious practice, light and fire have always been associated with the divine presence.

The evening prayer of the church was often called *lucernarium,* the service of light, or *hora lucernalis,* the hour of lights. The flame of the lamps signifies Christ, "the sun that never sets." The Latin word *vesper* originally meant an evening star. Then Vespers designated the prayer offered when the evening stars (vespers) started to appear. The chanting of the church's prayers at dusk was also called *hora incensi,* from the custom of burning incense at the time of the evening service. The psalmist prays in Psalm 141, "Let my prayer be counted as incense before you, and the lifting up of my hands as an evening sacrifice."

The chanting of psalms in the evening has its early roots in the temple sacrifices and prayers. Exodus mandates that the Israelites continually offer upon the altar two lambs every day: one lamb in the morning and another in the evening. The evening sacrifice was offered along with grain and wine, and it was accompanied by an incense offering. During the Exile, when the temple did not exist, and after the temple's destruction by Rome in A.D. 70, the synagogue services of psalms and readings from Scripture developed as a substitute for the animal sacrifices as a sacrifice of praise to the Lord.

According to the Torah, the day begins with the setting of the sun, as the creation account states: "There was evening and there was morning, the first day" (Gen 1:5). Because the day begins and ends at sundown according to the Torah, the feasts of Israel begin at sundown on the first day and end at nightfall on the last day. Christians continued this practice by beginning solemn feasts with the First Vespers prayed around sunset on the day before the observance, with Second Vespers held around sunset on the day itself.

As the church's morning prayer honors Christ's resurrection, evening prayer honors Christ's offering of himself at the Last Supper, which is completed at his death on the cross. As sunset approached, the body of Jesus was pierced, pouring forth the sacramental life of the church, and was laid in the tomb. The evening sacrifice of Christ fulfills the daily offering of the lamb at the temple and completes the descent of God into our humanity. In light of these saving events, Hebrews urges the church to "continually offer up a sacrifice of praise to God, that is, the fruit of lips that confess his name" (Heb 13:15).

Twilight is also associated with the onslaught of the Evil One—the temptation, sin, and death from which Christ came to set us free. The church's evening prayer is thus filled with confidence as we wait with joyful hope for the dawn, when the uncertain lamplight will lead to the perpetual light of Christ. When Christians gather to pray the psalms of the evening, joining in the solidarity of the church's liturgical prayer, they unite themselves with others throughout the world and throughout history, so that indeed, from the rising of the sun to its setting, the glory and honor of the Lord may be praised.

Reflection and discussion

- What are some of my thoughts, feelings, and moods associated with sunset?

- What would I need to change in order to turn to God in prayer at dusk? What might change in my life if I did?

Psalms of Trust and Confidence

The psalms of the evening are often characterized by trust in God. These prayers have arisen from people who have experienced a good deal of life, and they have more meaning for us after we've lived through some of life's tragic and exhilarating hours. Usually by midlife, we begin to experience signs of our mortality, and our ambitions have been tempered with reality; perhaps we've lost a dear one to death, or dreamed boldly only to see those dreams shattered by forces beyond our control.

The psalms of trust are not sung by people who have confidence in God because nothing significant has ever happened to them to disturb that trust. No, these psalms are the songs of people who have experienced the trials, sufferings, and failures of life, yet, looking back on it all, they realize that God has been with them. These psalms demonstrate a mature confidence, the trust of one who has lived through better and worse, sickness and health.

Even if we have not experienced as many of life's ups and downs as the psalmists, we can still relate their experiences to our own. The fears and disappointments and betrayals experienced by the poets find echoes in the experiences of each one of us—no matter how much or how little of life we've been through. The words of the psalms give us the words to express trust in God and give us confidence as we face the struggles ahead.

The trust of those who pray these psalms rests in the God of the covenant, the God who has proven trustworthy in the past and so can be trusted now. We have no reason to fear because the God who was with our ancestors is now with us. The faith of Israel rests on the remembrance of Exodus, as God chose and loved Israel although they had done nothing to earn or deserve that love. God heard the cries of Israel's pain and delivered his people from bondage, joining them in covenant, promising that he would be faithful to his people. God's promise to Moses, "I will be with you," became God's promise to all, betrothing himself to his bride Israel and promising her steadfast and faithful love.

This reality, renewed and confirmed over and over again throughout history, enables the daughters and sons of God to trust. Because of this faithful God, the psalmists can depend on God and look to the future with hope. Because of this trust, the people of God can direct words of praise, or thanks, or petition, or complaint to God.

The psalms of trust help us believe that nothing can take away God's faithful concern for us, that God is with us through thick and thin. The most powerful bond of love in human life is that which binds a parent and a child. But God's love for us is even stronger than that: "If my father and mother forsake me, the Lord will take me up" (Ps 27:10). Our God provides a home for us—the tent, the temple, the sanctuary, the dwelling where God abides with his children. In God's secure tent we find protection from all that seeks to harm us. The tent of Israel's wilderness journey became the temple of Jerusalem, the home address of God. This was the place where the people of God found their greatest peace. There was no greater joy for the Israelite than to go home to Jerusalem and go up to the temple of God.

It is hard for us to comprehend the place that Jerusalem and the temple occupied in the religious imagination of the Israelites. The temple is the place where heaven is in continuity with earth, where the Israelites could get a glimpse of paradise and sense something of the original relationship of humanity with God. The mystery of the transcendent and immanent God is focused in the temple. On the one hand, the Creator of the whole world cannot be localized in any finite space. As Solomon prayed at the temple's dedication, "Even heaven and the highest heaven cannot contain you, much less this house that I have built!" (1 Kings 8:27). Yet, God did indeed become present to the people of Israel when they came to the temple and worshipped. God took up residence with his people at this "dwelling place" of God.

Reflection and discussion

- Why would expressions of trust and confidence predominate the prayer of God's people in the evening?

- What are some of the images used by the psalmists to express confident assurance in God?

Poetic Imagery in the Psalms

In order to understand God's revelation in Scripture, we have to connect with the world of symbols and images. Since God is transcendent, far beyond our human capacity to know and understand, the only way we can talk about God is through human language. Through words that evoke images, we gain glimpses of who God is. So, the Bible, especially the psalms, is full of images of God and of our relationship to God.

Images and metaphors are far more powerful and expressive than abstract language. We can say God is righteous, or we can say, more vividly, God is a mighty fortress. We can say that God is compassionate, or we can say, more descriptively, God is a shepherd. We find countless examples of these divine metaphors throughout the psalms.

First, transcendent characterizations of God reflect the reality that God is far beyond the limits of ordinary experience. We say, for example, that God is the Creator, the giver of life, the Most High, and Lord. Second, human comparisons associate God with activities like those of a king, shepherd, judge, or parent. God's relationship to the psalmist is sometimes associated with the birthing process or maternal activities, as when the psalmist admits that his soul is as dependent before God as a "weaned child with its mother" (Ps 131:2). Such feminine imagery expands our understanding of the ways in which the divine and human are in relationship as well as reinforcing the sacredness of female sexuality. Third, animal analogies associate the qualities of God with the power, strength, and majesty of animals. For example, the image from Exodus, in which God says, "I bore you on eagles' wings," is evoked several times in the psalms, as when the psalmist chants, "[God] will cover you with his pinions, and under his wings you will find refuge" (Ps 91:4). And fourth, inanimate reality becomes a metaphor for God's qualities. God is water and light, a rock, a fortress, and a shield. "[God] alone is my rock and my salvation, my fortress; I shall not be shaken" (Ps 62:6).

There is no single portrait of God in the Bible. The God of Israel said, "I am who I am" (Exod 3:14). God is holy mystery, totally free and independent of human definition. God remains always free to be and to act in ways that are not predictable. Our God forbids us to ever make the divine according to our own image. This is the reason it is so seriously limiting to always describe God or imagine God in only one way. Whenever we limit God by associating God exclusively with a singular human image, we are bordering on the sin of idolatry. God is infinite mystery, but God is revealed in finite history in a plurality of ways.

Metaphors tell us something of who God is and how God acts. Yet, because there are so many images of God, the metaphors preserve the mystery of God. The many images of God allow us to relate to God in many ways, in different kinds of experiences. In this way, the psalms challenge us to break out of our limited notions of God, our too common ways of thinking about God. They stretch our imagination, allowing us to pray more richly and insightfully, because the mystery of God is more lavishly perceived. Growth in our relationship with God demands that we stretch our imagination, not fixing on the same image over and over again.

Although we relate to God through poetic images and metaphors, God is always more than we can imagine. The psalmists express their own understanding of God based on their own experience of God, but God is always much larger than any one psalmist can tell. So, we find throughout the psalms multiple conceptions of God. And this wide vision, this multitude of understandings, allows those who pray the psalms the freedom to express their own particular experience of relationship with God.

Reflection and discussion

- In what ways do I tend to limit my prayerful relationship with God by focusing on a narrow range of images and titles for God?

- What are some more of the images and titles of God throughout the Bible?

Praying the Psalms with the Church

Many hymns have evolved throughout the history of Christ's church, but there is one collection of songs, far older than the church, that has entwined itself in the church's practices from the beginning, interpreting its aspirations and enshrining its experiences. It is the poetry Jesus learned and chanted throughout his life, sang with his apostles on his last night while walking to Gethsemane, the verses he quoted while dying on the cross. This was the music that first sprang from the lips of the assembled disciples in Jerusalem as they gave joyful thanks in the midst of sorrow and persecution.

The early Christians gathered for morning and evening prayers, as they learned from their Jewish forebears. This fixed-hour prayer, along with the Eucharist, is the oldest surviving form of Christian spirituality. By the second and third centuries, as we know from the writings of Clement, Origen, and Tertullian, the observance of daily prayers in the morning and evening was the norm. These daily prayers were often said alone, though they could be offered by families or in small groups, yet they were never individualistic in nature. Rather, they employed the time-honored and time-polished recitations of the faith.

With the peace of Constantine in the fourth century, Christians could for the first time build churches and gather publicly to pray in them. The practice of public prayer in the morning and evening hours, grounded in the chanted psalms, spread throughout Palestine, Antioch, Constantinople, northern Africa, Spain, and elsewhere. A bishop or priest would lead the prayer, and the people would sing the psalms designated for dawn or dusk, learning them by heart along with their chanted tunes. Prayers and readings were added from other parts of the Bible, followed in some places by a brief homily. The service concluded with intercessions for the church's needs and a closing prayer.

At the same time, monastic life was developing, and the monks brought these fixed-hour prayers into their monasteries. As time passed, the people's practice waned and the chanting of psalms passed almost exclusively—

though never entirely—into the monasteries and became largely identified with the prayer of monks. Yet, gladly in recent decades, the Liturgy of the Hours, especially the prayers in the morning and evening, has become again the prayer of the whole church and has returned to cathedrals, parish churches, and dedicated communities throughout the world.

A common stumbling block to prayer is the inability to find the words for prayer, but the fixed-hour prayer of the psalms offers us a language for prayer. It offers us ancient wisdom that stretches back to before the time of Jesus. It conveys a wide range of feelings and concerns, offering a rich and nuanced vocabulary for prayer that deepens our ability to communicate with God throughout the day. Another block to cultivating a prayer life is the absence of a routine. Praying at fixed hours provides a prayer schedule, offering a consistent means of sanctifying the hours by praising God in the morning and thanking him in the evening.

The psalms offer us a refreshingly candid reflection of the human experience. The frank words express to God our joyful gratitude, deep despair, quiet hope, or vengeful rage. There is ample room in these scriptures for the whole messy range of human experience. They are big enough for all the human emotions in our inner world and outer world—all the various voices within us and in our world. When we are honest, we know there are parts of us that feel these raw, uncomfortable sentiments, parts that our more respectable selves often try to ignore and hide. The vivid, candid, even offensive language of the psalms grants permission for those less-polished parts of our humanity to be offered to God. The psalms give us a truthful voice where we can open up all those simmering feelings to God.

When we pray with the church, we don't necessarily need to personally feel the emotions expressed by the psalms because we are not praying these prayers only for ourselves. When the psalms we're praying don't match our inner state, we realize that there are people somewhere in the world feeling those emotions, and we can offer them to God on their behalf. Praying the psalms is not a private devotion; rather, we pray as part of the people of God and never alone. These ancient prayers pull me out of wherever I am internally and connect me with the whole world: with those suffering the effects of hurricanes and earthquakes, those who face daily poverty and war, the victims and perpetrators of all forms of violence, those bound by sickness and imprisonment.

When we pray the psalms with the church, we don't have to continually think about what words we're going to say next. We are free to fully enter into the act of praying, to participate in God's relationship with his people. This way of praying places us in a posture of openness to God, even if our mind wanders into our grocery list or weekend plans. It gradually restructures our mind and heart, sometimes working on us consciously and at other times subconsciously. Often we feel the change, but at times we simply trust that God is at work within us.

Praying the psalms reminds us that we are members of Christ's body, people of the church, in union with people around the globe, that we are praying for the life of the world with words used in countless languages over millennia to cry out to God. It's a way of loving the world, of offering up to God the joys, hopes, griefs, and anxieties of all people.

Reflection and discussion

- What are some of the differences between praying individualistically and praying with the church?

- What are some of the advantages of fixed-hour prayer over spontaneous prayer? Why do we need both?

Prayer

God Most High, you listen to the prayers of your people throughout each day and around the world. You have given us the prayerbook of your people in ancient Israel and of the church through the ages. Prepare my mind and heart to study these sacred texts so that I may grow in my ability to unite my life with the joys, hopes, griefs, and anxieties of your world. Guide my reading and meditation so that it leads me to prayer and witness, contributing ever more fully to Christ's reign on earth as in heaven. Keep me faithful during these weeks to the challenges that your word offers to me.

SUGGESTIONS FOR FACILITATORS, GROUP SESSION 1

1. If the group is meeting for the first time, or if there are newcomers joining the group, it is helpful to provide name tags.

2. Distribute the books to the members of the group.

3. You may want to ask the participants to introduce themselves and tell the group a bit about themselves.

4. Ask one or more of these introductory questions:
   - What drew you to join this group?
   - What is your biggest fear in beginning this Bible study?
   - How is beginning this study like a "threshold" for you?

5. You may want to pray this prayer as a group:
   Come upon us, Holy Spirit, to enlighten and guide us as we begin this study of the Psalms of the Evening. You inspired the authors of Scripture to reveal your presence throughout the history of salvation. This inspired word has the power to convert our hearts and change our lives. Fill our hearts with desire, trust, and confidence as you shine the light of your truth within us. Motivate us to read the Scriptures and give us a deeper love for God's word each day. Bless us during this session and throughout the coming week with the fire of your love.

6. Read the Introduction aloud, pausing at each question for discussion. Group members may wish to write down the insights of the group as each question is discussed. Encourage several members of the group to respond to each question.

7. Don't feel compelled to finish the complete Introduction during the session. It is better to allow sufficient time to talk about the questions raised than to rush to the end. Group members may read any remaining sections on their own after the group meeting.

8. Instruct group members to read the first six lessons on their own during the six days before the next group meeting. They should write out their own answers to the questions as preparation for next week's group discussion.

9. Fill in the date for each group meeting under "Schedule for Group Study."

10. Conclude by praying aloud together the prayer at the end of the Introduction.

LESSON 1 SESSION 2

The Lord is in his holy temple; the Lord's throne is in heaven.
His eyes behold, his gaze examines humankind.

PSALM 11:4

Confident Trust in the Lord's Presence

PSALM 11

1 *In the Lord I take refuge; how can you say to me,*
"Flee like a bird to the mountains;
2 *for look, the wicked bend the bow,*
they have fitted their arrow to the string,
to shoot in the dark at the upright in heart.
3 *If the foundations are destroyed,*
what can the righteous do?"

4 *The Lord is in his holy temple;*
the Lord's throne is in heaven.
His eyes behold, his gaze examines humankind.
5 *The Lord tests the righteous and the wicked,*
and his soul hates the lover of violence.
6 *On the wicked he will rain coals of fire and sulfur;*
a scorching wind shall be the portion of their cup.
7 *For the Lord is righteous;*
he loves righteous deeds;
the upright shall behold his face.

PSALM 15

1 *O Lord, who may abide in your tent?*
Who may dwell on your holy hill?

2 *Those who walk blamelessly, and do what is right,*
and speak the truth from their heart;
3 *who do not slander with their tongue,*
and do no evil to their friends,
nor take up a reproach against their neighbors;
4 *in whose eyes the wicked are despised,*
but who honor those who fear the Lord;
who stand by their oath even to their hurt;
5 *who do not lend money at interest,*
and do not take a bribe against the innocent.

Those who do these things shall never be moved.

In Psalm 11, the poet expresses trust in God, exclaiming, "In the Lord I take refuge," and encouraging listeners to be patient and confident under threat. The song expresses the confrontation between "the wicked" (11:2, 5, 6) and "the upright/righteous" (11:3, 5, 7). The threat of the wicked is developed with three images: a bird fleeing to the mountains, hunters drawing their bows to shoot in the dark, and shaking foundations that threaten to collapse.

The question that follows these images of threat, "What can the righteous do?" is answered with an image that promotes confidence: "The Lord is in his holy temple" (11:3–4). Our attention is averted from the terrifying images of flight, hunting, and collapse to the peaceful thought of the Lord enthroned in his dwelling, watching over humankind. This is the place whose foundations will never be destroyed. The temple in Jerusalem is the earthly model of God's heavenly temple. Although the copy may be destroyed, God's eternal dwelling will never crumble.

The Lord is enthroned as the righteous judge of the world. The basis on which "the Lord tests the righteous and the wicked" is not a moral code but is his own character and preferences. The Lord is himself righteous, and therefore "he loves righteous deeds" and "hates the lover of violence" (11:5–7). People are judged not by how they regard God but by how they behave toward other people, whether with violence or justice. Although the wicked are punished for their rejection of God's ways, the righteous behold the face of God in his heavenly temple.

Psalm 15 opens with the poet's questions, addressed to those seeking to enter the place where God dwells. The "tent" of God's presence in the wilderness became the sanctuary in Jerusalem, and the "holy hill" became the sacred city with its temple (15:1). The answer to the question "Who?" takes the form of an oracle of instruction, listing a series of positive and negative qualifications. Some of these involve living rightly and avoiding evil. Others focus on speech, like speaking the truth and avoiding slanderous insults and false accusations of others (15:2–3).

Personal integrity, in both speech and action, is essential for those who wish to dwell with God. They must watch the company they keep, siding with God's friends, "those who fear the Lord," against "the wicked." They must "stand by their oath," "not lend money at interest," and "not take a bribe against the innocent" (15:4–5). An oath is a promise to others that must be kept, despite inconvenience or personal loss. Lending money with interest takes advantage of the poor and gains power and control over others. And taking a bribe perverts the system of justice for personal gain. All of these are means of acquiring wealth and influence, placing self-interest over the legitimate interests of others.

The final phrase of the psalm offers the assurance that those who live in this way will certainly dwell in the Lord's abiding presence. They "shall never be moved" because the foundations of God's place of dwelling will never crumble and fall. They may rest secure and confident in his presence. Indeed, they may trust in the Lord.

Reflection and discussion

- What are the similar images and messages of these two psalms?

- In what people, institutions, or possessions do I seek to trust, rather than in God alone?

- Which words of each psalm help me to trust confidently in God?

Prayer

Lord God, you dwell in your heavenly temple and care for the people of the earth. May I live in such a way as to be counted among the righteous who long to behold your face. Help me to trust not in worldly riches and power but in your unshakable dwelling.

I bless the Lord who gives me counsel; in the night also my heart instructs me. I keep the Lord always before me; because he is at my right hand, I shall not be moved. PSALM 16:7–8

Seeking the Path to Life

PSALM 16

1*Protect me, O God, for in you I take refuge.*
2*I say to the Lord, "You are my Lord;*
I have no good apart from you."

3*As for the holy ones in the land, they are the noble,*
in whom is all my delight.

4*Those who choose another god multiply their sorrows;*
their drink offerings of blood I will not pour out
or take their names upon my lips.

5*The Lord is my chosen portion and my cup;*
you hold my lot.
6*The boundary lines have fallen for me in pleasant places;*
I have a goodly heritage.

7*I bless the Lord who gives me counsel;*
in the night also my heart instructs me.
8*I keep the Lord always before me;*
because he is at my right hand, I shall not be moved.

9*Therefore my heart is glad, and my soul rejoices;*
my body also rests secure.
10*For you do not give me up to Sheol,*
or let your faithful one see the Pit.

[11]*You show me the path of life.*
In your presence there is fullness of joy;
in your right hand are pleasures forevermore.

The psalm articulates a supreme and increasingly personal sense of trust in God. Beginning with a plea for safety and security, "Protect me, O God, for in you I take refuge," the poet entrusts his life to God's care as his shelter from harm (verse 1). The rest of the psalm explores this confident trust in God, which is not just a tender feeling but the continual choice of God and regular practices that deepen one's consciousness of the Lord as life's ultimate good. The poet knows that his life belongs to God, declaring, "You are my Lord" (verse 2). As God's servant, he knows that everything that is given to him comes from his Lord. Every verse of the psalm, in one way or another, expresses this grateful expression: "I have no good apart from you." God is the shelter, destiny, heritage, advisor, security, and guide for the one who trusts supremely in the Lord.

Trust in God entails focused and exclusive commitment (verses 3–4). There can be no other God besides the Lord. All the other deities worshiped in the land are only sources of trouble. Those who multiply their gods also multiply their sorrows. The poet pledges never to honor them, neither in word nor in sacrifice.

Instead, the psalmist declares that the Lord is his portion and cup, the one who holds his lot (verses 5–6). Using images from the book of Joshua, describing the apportionment of the promised land to the tribes and clans of Israel, the poet asserts that his relationship with God is his greatest provision. He knows that the boundary lines have been determined by God, who has measured out the allocation of each. The poet gratefully acknowledges that his own designated share has provided him with a pleasant location and a substantial inheritance.

Maintaining confident trust in God means keeping him at the center of one's attention, continually enjoying the divine presence (verses 7–8). In this way, the psalmist is able to be open to the Lord's guidance, which comes to him through the prompting of his heart, even in the darkness of night, temptation, or threat. With the Lord next to him, at his "right hand," he remains faithful and true. "I shall not be moved," he declares, affirming that he cannot be threatened or unsettled by anything less than God.

Trust in God is manifested in all three dimensions of the poet's being: his heart, soul, and body (verse 9). Confidence in the abiding presence of God infuses his entire self and is the source of his joy and security. Such total conviction is even stronger than death (verses 10–11). God does not allow his faithful one to be surrendered to the shadows of the underworld or the pit of destruction. Rather, God shows his trusting servant the "path of life," the way to live with the everlasting joy of God's presence.

The psalms may be understood in a variety of ways, depending on who is praying it and in what situation. An individual Israelite may chant this psalm to the Lord, seeking refuge in the temple from a threat of enemies or untimely death. The psalm may also be a prayer of corporate Israel, perhaps following the Exile, asking God to protect them from further harm and bless them with confidence.

In the early church, we know that this psalm was prayed in the light of Christ's resurrection. Peter quoted the psalm in his address to the crowd at the feast of Pentecost (Acts 2:24–32). Likewise, Paul quoted this psalm in his speech at Antioch of Pisidia, indicating that the resurrection fulfills God's promises made to their ancestors (Acts 13:35–37). Both apostles gave confidence to their listeners by enabling them to pray this psalm with complete trust. In Jesus Christ is found "the path of life" and the "fullness of joy."

Reflection and discussion

- What prevents me from trusting God completely?

- What difference does it make when I pray this psalm in light of Christ's resurrection?

Prayer

Lord God, my portion and my cup, you are the only true God and the only source of lasting happiness, counsel, and security. Help me to place all my trust in you, for in you is found the path of life and the fullness of joy forever.

He asked you for life; you gave it to him—length of days forever and ever. His glory is great through your help; splendor and majesty you bestow on him. PSALM 21:4–5

Petition and Thanksgiving for the King's Victory

PSALM 20

1 *The Lord answer you in the day of trouble!*
The name of the God of Jacob protect you!
2 *May he send you help from the sanctuary,*
and give you support from Zion.
3 *May he remember all your offerings,*
and regard with favor your burnt sacrifices. Selah

4 *May he grant you your heart's desire,*
and fulfill all your plans.
5 *May we shout for joy over your victory,*
and in the name of our God set up our banners.
May the Lord fulfill all your petitions.

6 *Now I know that the Lord will help his anointed;*
he will answer him from his holy heaven
with mighty victories by his right hand.
7 *Some take pride in chariots, and some in horses,*
but our pride is in the name of the Lord our God.
8 *They will collapse and fall,*
but we shall rise and stand upright.

9 *Give victory to the king, O Lord;*
answer us when we call.

PSALM 21

1 *In your strength the king rejoices, O Lord,*
and in your help how greatly he exults!
2 *You have given him his heart's desire,*
and have not withheld the request of his lips. Selah
3 *For you meet him with rich blessings;*
you set a crown of fine gold on his head.
4 *He asked you for life; you gave it to him—*
length of days forever and ever.
5 *His glory is great through your help;*
splendor and majesty you bestow on him.
6 *You bestow on him blessings forever;*
you make him glad with the joy of your presence.
7 *For the king trusts in the Lord,*
and through the steadfast love of the Most High he shall not be moved.

8 *Your hand will find out all your enemies;*
your right hand will find out those who hate you.
9 *You will make them like a fiery furnace*
when you appear.
The Lord will swallow them up in his wrath,
and fire will consume them.
10 *You will destroy their offspring from the earth,*
and their children from among humankind.
11 *If they plan evil against you,*
if they devise mischief, they will not succeed.
12 *For you will put them to flight;*
you will aim at their faces with your bows.

13 *Be exalted, O Lord, in your strength!*
We will sing and praise your power.

Both of these are royal psalms: Psalm 20 is a prayer for the king before battle, and Psalm 21 is a thanksgiving after the king's victory. The invocation in the first psalm, "May he grant you your heart's desire" (20:4), is shown to be answered in the next: "You have given him his heart's desire" (21:2). Both psalms testify that the authority of Israel's king originates in God; therefore, the king must honor his obligations before God and trust in the Lord for all his strength.

Psalm 20 begins by addressing the king, imploring God's help and protection upon him. The "name" of God, a divine manifestation bearing the presence and power of God, is invoked to rally the people and army of the nation (20:1, 5, 7). References to the sanctuary on Zion and the king's offerings and sacrifices testify to the importance of the temple rituals (20:2–3). Yet, the king's offerings to God are expressions of devotion, not attempts to manipulate God to grant the prayer's request. God's acceptance is petitioned, not presumed, asking that God remember and regard them with favor. The king represents the people in the sense that his desires and plans are for the sake of the people (20:4–5). His victory will lead to their joyful celebration, and their celebration gives honor to the name of God.

The psalm shifts from prayers of petition to a prayer of confident trust, with the psalmist speaking on behalf of the congregation: "Now I know that the Lord will help his anointed" (20:6). In response to the earlier petition for God's help from the sanctuary on Zion, the psalm voices assurance that the Lord will answer his anointed king "from his holy heaven." The temple on Zion is God's dwelling place in the midst of his people, but it also symbolizes God's dwelling in heaven. In the temple and its rituals, the king and his people experience God's presence and invoke his help from his heavenly abode. The truest source of their victory is not in their own chariots, horses, and military power but in the superior power of the Lord (20:7–8). And the consequence of this confident faith is evident: the enemies "will collapse and fall," while Israel "shall rise and stand upright."

The summarizing final verse is directed to God (20:9). It expresses something essential about the relationship between the Lord, the king, the people, and the liturgical prayers at the temple. The voicing of confident trust, "I know that the Lord will help his anointed," does not ensure that it will be realized. Whether the Lord will "give victory to the king" depends ultimately on the relationship of the king and his people with God. The people plead, "Answer us when we call." The victory is dependent on the heavenly king, not the earthly one. Human power and prestige cannot save; God alone can deliver his people.

The trusting petitions of Psalm 20 give way to the praise and thanksgiving of Psalm 21. God is directly addressed by the psalmist, but the subject is the king. The hymn emphatically underlines the dependence of the king on the strength and help of the Lord (21:1–6). All the king's "blessings"—his deep desires, length of life, glory, splendor, and majesty—are due to God. These blessings derive from the king's prayerful and intimate relationship with the Lord.

In a transitional verse, the psalmist addresses the congregation in order to state the reasons for God's abundant blessings on the king. They are due to the interaction of the king's trust in the Lord and the Lord's faithful love for the king (21:7). The divine title, Most High, reminds the king and the people of the hierarchy of power, and God's "steadfast love" echoes the royal covenant God made with David and his lineage on the throne. Because of God's promise, his king "shall not be moved," for he is settled on the throne of David and his descendants.

The psalm then shifts to an extended oracle addressed to the king (21:8–12). Its purpose is to give confidence to the king and people of future victories over their enemies. Although this oracle could refer to future military battles, its meaning is most fully understood as spiritual warfare, the struggle against the powers of sin and evil fought by God's anointed king.

As with Psalm 20, this psalm ends with a petition addressed to God (21:13). Although the psalm has celebrated the king's success, clearly the Lord is the one who must be ultimately exalted and praised. It is God's strength and power that must be acclaimed over all.

The Jewish people continued to pray these psalms long after the period of the monarchy in Jerusalem. Through these prayers they continued to await the coming Messiah, the anointed one of God. Christians understood that the prayers of these psalms were completed by Jesus Christ, the King of kings. In him the name of the Lord is fully revealed, and he offers the perfect sacrifice in which he himself is the victim. In his defeat of the inimical powers of sin and death, he gains the victory. In his resurrection, the Father has given him the fullness of life, length of days forever and ever. He is invested with splendor and majesty, and he rejoices in the Father's presence. With our spiritual ancestors in Israel, who sang of the steadfast love of the Most High, we can now praise the power of Christ our King, knowing that we are destined to share forever in his glorious victory.

Reflection and discussion

- In what way is trust in military weapons a contradiction to faith in the Lord?

- Is it easier for me to pray these psalms when focusing on a cosmic battlefield, struggling against the spiritual enemies of evil and sin?

- What difference does it make when praying these psalms when I realize that Christ is the truest king who has gained ultimate victory for us all?

Prayer

God Most High, give me confidence in your steadfast love. Through your anointed Son, give me victory over the powers of evil, sin, and death so that we may experience your every spiritual blessing.

"Come," my heart says, "seek his face!" Your face, Lord, do I seek. Do not hide your face from me. PSALM 27:8–9

Moving from Fear to Trust

PSALM 27

1 *The Lord is my light and my salvation;*
whom shall I fear?
The Lord is the stronghold of my life;
of whom shall I be afraid?

2 *When evildoers assail me*
to devour my flesh—
my adversaries and foes—
they shall stumble and fall.

3 *Though an army encamp against me,*
my heart shall not fear;
though war rise up against me,
yet I will be confident.

4 *One thing I asked of the Lord,*
that will I seek after:
to live in the house of the Lord
all the days of my life,
to behold the beauty of the Lord,
and to inquire in his temple.

5 *For he will hide me in his shelter*
in the day of trouble;
he will conceal me under the cover of his tent;
he will set me high on a rock.

6 *Now my head is lifted up*
above my enemies all around me,
and I will offer in his tent
sacrifices with shouts of joy;
I will sing and make melody to the Lord.

7 *Hear, O Lord, when I cry aloud,*
be gracious to me and answer me!
8 *"Come," my heart says, "seek his face!"*
Your face, Lord, do I seek.
9 *Do not hide your face from me.*

Do not turn your servant away in anger,
you who have been my help.
Do not cast me off, do not forsake me,
O God of my salvation!
10 *If my father and mother forsake me,*
the Lord will take me up.

11 *Teach me your way, O Lord,*
and lead me on a level path
because of my enemies.
12 *Do not give me up to the will of my adversaries,*
for false witnesses have risen against me,
and they are breathing out violence.

13 *I believe that I shall see the goodness of the Lord*
in the land of the living.
14 *Wait for the Lord;*
be strong, and let your heart take courage;
wait for the Lord!

Whom do I fear? Of whom am I afraid? Fear is a reality throughout everyone's life. Some of our childhood fears were of darkness or of being alone. Those same fears take different forms as we grow older. The fear of darkness is replaced by the fear of leading a meaningless life. The fear of being alone is replaced by the fear of being without someone to love. We are afraid of not having control of our lives; we are afraid of the powers of nature; we fear death; we fear being rejected. Psychologists have diagnosed hundreds of different types of phobias—conscious or subconscious fears that prevent a person from trusting life and responding to reality with confidence. We have no idea how our inner fears can prevent us from living fully.

The constant refrain of God throughout the Scriptures is "Do not be afraid." This psalm is designed to help those who live in fear and move them toward a life of trust. The poet begins with declarations about God: "my light," "my salvation," "the stronghold of my life" (verse 1). The Lord illumines, protects, saves, and dispels fear. The source of the psalmist's fears are represented by "evildoers," who are described as ravenous animals, "adversaries and foes," who are bound to fall (verse 2). Even under the attack of a hostile army waging war, the poet asserts his confident trust (verse 3).

This trust in the Lord leads the psalmist to declare that his one request in times of fear is to live in the presence of God (verses 4–6). This divine presence is expressed through images of the temple, the place of God's dwelling. There, in the sanctuary, he will be sheltered in time of trouble. Concealed in the Lord's tent and set high on a rock, the psalmist will be protected from the enemies surrounding him. There he can worship God without fear, offering sacrifices and singing psalms. These tender images of dwelling with God and giving him joyful praise evoke emotions of comfort and security.

At the psalm's midpoint, the tone changes and the song becomes a prayer addressed to God (verses 7–12). The psalmist prays that the Lord hear his cry and answer his needs, complementing the confident confession of trust in the psalm's first half. Trust becomes real and active in the face of life's threats, when one experiences vulnerability and helplessness. It is then that anxious fear is transformed into genuine prayer.

The poet desires to seek God's presence, begging, "Do not hide your face from me" (verses 8–9). Crying out, "O God of my salvation!" he fears being turned away and forsaken by God. Yet, he knows that his relationship with the Lord is more reliable and enduring than even that of father and mother (verse 10). Adversity may drive a father or mother to forsake their role as parents, but it moves God all the more to respond to his servant. The psalmist prays that God teach him and lead him, that God not give him over to his enemies who are giving false witness about him and threatening violence (verse

11–12). In ancient Israel, as in all societies, lying words are dangerous. False testimony could lead its victim into exclusion, captivity, and execution.

The psalm concludes with a reaffirmation of trust in God (verses 13–14). The poet expresses confidence in God's goodness, both for himself and in witness to others who find themselves in similar desperation. Urging others to be determined and courageous in the face of fear, the psalmist exhorts, "Wait for the Lord." Bound and strengthened by our shared experiences of fear and salvation, we hope in God together.

Because the images and emotions of the psalms cannot be bound to any one individual or historical circumstance, they have invited readers in every age to understand their own circumstances as closely tied to those of the psalmist. So, in situations of fear and trial, we can call out to God through the words of this psalm of trust. Opposition, verbal assaults, false accusation, and insult pervade the history of God's people, from the prophets, to Jesus the Messiah, to Paul and the martyrs. The psalm expresses the virtue of trust for those living a way of life that will again and again be misrepresented and slurred by those who fail to understand it. Yet, God's faithful can move from fear to trust.

Reflection and discussion

- What is the one fear I just can't seem to overcome?

- If I could ask of the Lord "one thing," what would it be? Why not ask for it now?

Prayer

O God of my salvation, do not forsake your servant who calls to you. Teach me your way and lead me on your path, that I may conquer my fears and trust in you with greater confidence and courage.

For his anger is but for a moment; his favor is for a lifetime.
Weeping may linger for the night, but joy comes with the morning.
PSALM 30:5

Thanksgiving for Deliverance and Forgiveness

PSALM 30

1 *I will extol you, O Lord, for you have drawn me up,*
and did not let my foes rejoice over me.
2 *O Lord my God, I cried to you for help,*
and you have healed me.
3 *O Lord, you brought up my soul from Sheol,*
restored me to life from among those gone down to the Pit.

4 *Sing praises to the Lord, O you his faithful ones,*
and give thanks to his holy name.
5 *For his anger is but for a moment;*
his favor is for a lifetime.
Weeping may linger for the night,
but joy comes with the morning.

6 *As for me, I said in my prosperity,*
"I shall never be moved."
7 *By your favor, O Lord,*
you had established me as a strong mountain;
you hid your face;
I was dismayed.

8 *To you, O Lord, I cried,*
and to the Lord I made supplication:
9 *"What profit is there in my death,*
if I go down to the Pit?
Will the dust praise you?
Will it tell of your faithfulness?
10 *Hear, O Lord, and be gracious to me!*
O Lord, be my helper!"

11 *You have turned my mourning into dancing;*
you have taken off my sackcloth
and clothed me with joy,
12 *so that my soul may praise you and not be silent.*
O Lord my God, I will give thanks to you forever.

PSALM 32

1 *Happy are those whose transgression is forgiven,*
whose sin is covered.
2 *Happy are those to whom the Lord imputes no iniquity,*
and in whose spirit there is no deceit.

3 *While I kept silence, my body wasted away*
through my groaning all day long.
4 *For day and night your hand was heavy upon me;*
my strength was dried up as by the heat of summer. Selah

5 *Then I acknowledged my sin to you,*
and I did not hide my iniquity;
I said, "I will confess my transgressions to the Lord,"
and you forgave the guilt of my sin. Selah

6 *Therefore let all who are faithful*
offer prayer to you;
at a time of distress, the rush of mighty waters
shall not reach them.
7 *You are a hiding place for me;*
you preserve me from trouble;
you surround me with glad cries of deliverance. Selah

8 I will instruct you and teach you the way you should go;
I will counsel you with my eye upon you.
9 Do not be like a horse or a mule, without understanding,
whose temper must be curbed with bit and bridle,
else it will not stay near you.

10 Many are the torments of the wicked,
but steadfast love surrounds those who trust in the Lord.
11 Be glad in the Lord and rejoice, O righteous,
and shout for joy, all you upright in heart.

Psalm 30 is a song offering thanksgiving to God. The psalmist has been rescued by God from a situation of great distress. The nature of the trial is not specified, allowing the psalm to express gratitude to God for any number of saving experiences. Its structure consists of a series of contrasts: death and silence versus life and praise.

The psalm opens as the speaker exalts God who has lifted him up from the assault of his foes (30:1–3). As the psalmist narrates his experience in the form of a prayer to God, he describes his cry for help and his healing from God. He describes his experience as going down into "Sheol," the shadowy underworld of the dead, to "the Pit," the deep prison of those who are doomed. The verses are a series of reversals: he cried out for help and God healed him; he was going down to destruction, but God brought him up from ruin.

The psalmist's grateful praise is not a private matter with God, but it ought to be sung by God's "faithful ones" (30:4–6). The singer's distress and deliverance serve as an example of what God can do for all. He describes God's initiative: "His anger is but for a moment; his favor is for a lifetime." Divine anger is distinguished from divine favor; one is momentary and the other is lifelong. Then he expresses the human response to God's saving acts: "Weeping may linger for the night, but joy comes with the morning." Weeping is contrasted with joy; the night with the morning. Life is clearly a series of ups and downs. The Lord is not a God who preserves his people from hardships but one who delivers them from ruin.

The psalmist recalls his overconfidence during the days of his prosperity, when he assumed that God's favor had established him as sturdy as an unmovable mountain (30:6–7). Yet, when God's favor was withdrawn, his fortune turned to folly. His dismay forced him to recognize his need for God's mercy, so he cried out in supplication (30:8–10). With straightforward sincerity, the psalmist essentially asks God, "Who will offer you praise if you allow me to die?"

After pleading for God's help, the psalmist offers thanks to God for reversing his fortune with divine blessing (verses 11–12). God has turned his mourning into dancing, and he has removed his sackcloth and clothed him with joy. Rather than experiencing the silence of death, his soul will praise God and give him thanks forever. The transformation from illness to healing, from weeping to joy, from confusion to certainty, from silence to praise, from fear to trust, from imminent death to new life all encompass experiences of God's redeeming grace in our lives.

Psalm 32 is also a song of thanksgiving which includes a typical narration of trouble, followed by an appeal to the Lord, and then deliverance from harm. But first, the psalmist pronounces a blessing on those who, like himself, are forgiven by God (32:1–2). His prayer offers public testimony to encourage others to a spirit of penitence. Those whose transgressions are confessed and pardoned are freed from deceitfulness, and thus they are able to give God thanks and praise.

Narrating his own time of distress, the psalmist testifies that he "kept silence" about his sin, causing emotional and even bodily anguish (32:3–4). But then, he admits that he "acknowledged" his wrong and "did not hide" his iniquity. When he decided to "confess" his sins to God, then God "forgave" his guilt (32:5). Confession of sins is not a matter of secret remorse or therapeutic self-talk. As when one has wronged a spouse, parent, or friend, the offense must be put into words when forgiveness is sought. With God, too, the silence must be broken and the contrition expressed.

As the psalmist continues his grateful narrative, he does so as an invitation to others, encouraging the practice of penitence to those who are faithful to the covenant (32:6–7). For those who pray, God will deliver them from the rushing waters of overwhelming distress, and God's presence will become for them a "hiding place" to preserve them from trouble.

The psalmist is an individual who has been delivered by God from the effects of iniquity but also a representational figure embodying the experience of God's people making their way from sin to deliverance. As such, the psalmist becomes a guide for others: "I will instruct you and teach you the way you should go; I will counsel you with my eye upon you" (32:8–9). The listeners are warned not to be like the horse or mule, not understanding instructions and refusing to go in the way they should go.

A memorable maxim closes this hymn of grateful praise (32:10–11). The woes of the wicked are contrasted with God's faithful love that surrounds those who live with trust. These are the ones who may be glad, rejoice, and shout for joy because their transgressions are forgiven.

Reflection and discussion

- What reversal of fortune has allowed me to experience God's redeeming grace?

- How is it possible to confess sins with integrity, in such a way that "there is no deceit"? Can God be deceived, or can sinners deceive themselves?

- Why does the psalmist urge the listeners to verbally confess their transgressions to the Lord? What are some of the effects of unacknowledged sin?

Prayer

O Lord my God, your mercy is always upon me whenever I turn to you for deliverance from destruction and whenever I confess my sins to seek your forgiveness. Turn my mourning into dancing and my silence into rejoicing.

Even my bosom friend in whom I trusted, who ate of my bread, has lifted the heel against me. But you, O Lord, be gracious to me, and raise me up, that I may repay them. PSALM 41:9–10

Instructions on the Way to Happiness

PSALM 41

1 *Happy are those who consider the poor;*
the Lord delivers them in the day of trouble.
2 *The Lord protects them and keeps them alive;*
they are called happy in the land.
You do not give them up to the will of their enemies.
3 *The Lord sustains them on their sickbed;*
in their illness you heal all their infirmities.

4 *As for me, I said, "O Lord, be gracious to me;*
heal me, for I have sinned against you."
5 *My enemies wonder in malice*
when I will die, and my name perish.
6 *And when they come to see me, they utter empty words,*
while their hearts gather mischief;
when they go out, they tell it abroad.
7 *All who hate me whisper together about me;*
they imagine the worst for me.

8 *They think that a deadly thing has fastened on me,*
that I will not rise again from where I lie.
9 *Even my bosom friend in whom I trusted,*
who ate of my bread, has lifted the heel against me.

10 *But you, O Lord, be gracious to me,*
and raise me up, that I may repay them.

11 *By this I know that you are pleased with me;*
because my enemy has not triumphed over me.
12 *But you have upheld me because of my integrity,*
and set me in your presence forever.

13 *Blessed be the Lord, the God of Israel,*
from everlasting to everlasting.
Amen and Amen.

This instructive psalm begins with an extended beatitude describing God's approval, help, and blessing for those who are concerned about the poor (verses 1–3). Care for the weak, the needy, and the helpless is the concern of God, so it should also be the concern of God's people. Those who consider the poor will likewise be cared for by God in the day of their trouble. They will be protected from their enemies and healed in their sicknesses. This lesson is taught by the Torah, prophets, and wisdom of the ancient Scriptures, and Jesus himself both taught and exemplified this truth: "Blessed are the merciful, for they will receive mercy" (Matt 5:7). Jesus identified himself with the weak and helpless and suffered the rejection they experienced.

The psalmist then narrates his own experience, describing his prayer to God in his time of trouble. He begins and ends his lament by crying to God for mercy: "O Lord, be gracious to me" (verses 4, 10). He seeks both physical healing of recovery from sickness as well as the spiritual healing that comes from forgiveness of sins. Yet, his enemies believe he has been struck with a deadly misfortune and will not recover (verses 5–8). The vocabulary is filled with sickness and hostility. The illness stirs repulsion rather than compassion. They fully expect that he will die and his memory be forgotten. Those who visit him "utter empty words," courteous platitudes, and then in public whisper idle gossip, imagining the worst. Even his trusted friend, who shared meals with him, has "lifted the heel" against him, turning away in his time of need (verse 9). Jesus quoted these words about his own friend Judas: "The one who ate my bread has lifted his heel against me" (John 13:18).

The psalm's description of sickness is realistic as it describes the reactions of friends, acquaintances, and enemies. Illnesses isolate patients both physically and emotionally. They imagine themselves a burden and feel that it would perhaps be better to die. They often listen to empty words rather than experience the gift of compassionate presence. Those who believe that the death of the sick one is only a matter of time can be especially dismissive.

Nonetheless, the psalm concludes with a prayer of gratitude that the appeal for healing has been answered (verses 11–13). The enemies have not triumphed, but rather the truth of the opening beatitude has been affirmed. God is given praise, and the faith of the listeners is fortified. The reason God has upheld the psalmist in his struggle is his "integrity," the psalmist's desire to embody God's teaching in practice. God has granted him pardon and healing, set him in the divine presence, and restored him to the life of the community and the worship of God's people.

Reflection and discussion

- Why do people sometimes assume that there is not much to be learned from the poor or not much value in helping them?

- Why is betrayal by a close friend such an egregious offense? What do I hear in this psalm when I imagine Jesus and his mystical body on earth offering the prayer?

Prayer

O Lord, be gracious to me, in my times of trouble. Raise me up and do not let the deception of my friends or the assaults of my enemies overwhelm me. Set me in your presence and let me give you grateful praise all my days.

SUGGESTIONS FOR FACILITATORS, GROUP SESSION 2

1. If there are newcomers who were not present for the first group session, introduce them now.

2. You may want to pray this prayer as a group:
   God Most High, help us conquer our fears and trust in you with greater confidence and courage. We know that you are the only true God and our only source of lasting happiness, counsel, and security. Your mercy is always upon us whenever we turn to you for deliverance from harm and whenever we confess our sins to seek your forgiveness. Turn our silence into rejoicing, our anxiety into gratitude, and our mourning into dancing. May we live in such a way as to be counted among those who yearn for your unshakable dwelling and long to behold your face.

3. Ask one or both of the following questions:
   - What was your biggest challenge in Bible study over this past week?
   - What did you learn about yourself this week?

4. Discuss lessons 1 through 6 together. Assuming that group members have read the Scripture and commentary during the week, there is no need to read it aloud. As you review each lesson, you might want to briefly summarize the Scripture passages of each lesson and ask the group what stands out most clearly from the commentary.

5. Choose one or more of the questions for reflection and discussion from each lesson to talk over as a group. You may want to ask group members which question was most challenging or helpful to them as you review each lesson.

6. Keep the discussion moving, but don't rush it in order to complete more questions. Allow time for the questions that provoke the most discussion.

7. Instruct group members to complete lessons 7 through 12 on their own during the six days before the next group meeting. They should write out their own answers to the questions as preparation for next week's group discussion.

8. Conclude by praying aloud together the prayer at the end of lesson 6 or any other prayer you choose.

The princess is decked in her chamber with gold-woven robes; in many-colored robes she is led to the king; behind her the virgins, her companions, follow. PSALM 45:13–14

Song for the Royal Marriage

PSALM 45

1 *My heart overflows with a goodly theme;*
I address my verses to the king;
my tongue is like the pen of a ready scribe.

2 *You are the most handsome of men;*
grace is poured upon your lips;
therefore God has blessed you forever.
3 *Gird your sword on your thigh, O mighty one,*
in your glory and majesty.

4 *In your majesty ride on victoriously*
for the cause of truth and to defend the right;
let your right hand teach you dread deeds.
5 *Your arrows are sharp*
in the heart of the king's enemies;
the peoples fall under you.

6 *Your throne, O God, endures forever and ever.*
Your royal scepter is a scepter of equity;
7 *you love righteousness and hate wickedness.*
Therefore God, your God, has anointed you
with the oil of gladness beyond your companions;
8 *your robes are all fragrant with myrrh and aloes and cassia.*
From ivory palaces stringed instruments make you glad;

9daughters of kings are among your ladies of honor;
at your right hand stands the queen in gold of Ophir.

10Hear, O daughter, consider and incline your ear;
forget your people and your father's house,
11and the king will desire your beauty.
Since he is your lord, bow to him;
12the people of Tyre will seek your favor with gifts,
the richest of the people 13with all kinds of wealth.

The princess is decked in her chamber with gold-woven robes;
14in many-colored robes she is led to the king;
behind her the virgins, her companions, follow.
15With joy and gladness they are led along
as they enter the palace of the king.

16In the place of ancestors you, O king, shall have sons;
you will make them princes in all the earth.
17I will cause your name to be celebrated in all generations;
therefore the peoples will praise you forever and ever.

Composed as a wedding song for a royal groom and bride as they celebrated their marriage, this psalm expresses the elaborateness of the event. In Israel's culture, the royal wedding was both a religious and political event, since the monarch played the central role in both spheres. The psalm opens and closes with the voice of the composer, who describes his composition as his own heartfelt verses for the king, to be always remembered by his people (verses 1, 17). His tongue, he says, is "like the pen of a ready scribe," reminding us of the originally oral nature of the composition and performance of the psalms.

The first section addresses the royal groom, acclaiming him as an ideal ruler: he is handsome, articulate, and blessed by God (verses 2–9). Attired for battle, with his sword on his thigh, he is mighty, glorious, and majestic. He fights "for the cause of truth and to defend the right," emphasizing the moral qualities that characterize his rule. With sharp arrows he defeats his enemies and saves the kingdom.

The throne of the king represents the throne of God, hence the one who sits on the throne is ambiguous in the phrase "Your throne, O God, endures forever and ever" (verse 6). The king of the lineage of David represents God to the people and is addressed as God's royal son. He is said to "love righteousness and hate wickedness" because the scepter of God's kingdom is a "scepter of equity" (verse 7). The sword and the scepter represent two royal responsibilities: to fend off aggression and administer justice.

The most essential part of the coronation ritual of a new king is the anointing with oil. This ancient ritual expresses the conferment of divine blessing, indicating that the king is ruling on behalf of God. He is clothed in robes fragrant with the richest spices of the east. Music enlivens the ivory-inlaid rooms of the palace. The daughters of foreign kings accompany his royal harem, and "the queen," the mother of the king, stands in golden dress to the right of her royal son (verse 9).

The next section addresses the royal bride: first offering her advice as the wife of the monarch, then providing an eloquent description of how she will look as she is led into the chamber of her husband (verses 10–15). Because she is a princess from a foreign country, she is advised to put behind her any desire to return to her homeland and the court of her father. She must focus new life on her husband's realm and recognize that her spouse is also her king. She is wooed with promises of devotion, wealth, and renown.

The bride is clothed in robes woven with gold and dyed in many colors; her virgin companions follow behind her. She is joyfully led into the palace for presentation to the king and for the consummation of the union (verses 13–16). Again, the psalmist addresses the king, assuring him of the blessings of posterity. In a final flourish, the psalmist boasts, "I will cause your name to be celebrated in all generations" (verse 17).

When there was no longer a king in ancient Israel, Jewish interpreters began to understand this psalm in reference to the future Messiah. Likewise, Christian interpreters have understood the psalm as addressed to Christ and to his bride, the church. The psalmist applies to the king expressions that are elsewhere used for God: "glory and majesty," the "dread deeds" of his right hand, a divine throne that "endures forever and ever," a royal scepter of justice for the one who is said to "love righteousness and hate wickedness." Of course, these passages come to their fullness in Jesus, the royal

Messiah. This anointed one of God embodies within himself both divine and human identity.

Reflection and discussion

- What are the most appealing qualities of the bride and groom?

- How does someone truly loving me help me "forget" all other relationships?

- What are some of the things from my past that I must "forget" in order to truly honor Jesus Christ as my Lord?

Prayer

Lord God, you have anointed your Son as the Messiah of Israel and appointed him as the royal Bridegroom. Help me disregard any other relationships that prevent me from holding him as my King and Lord and guide me into the blessed joy of your kingdom.

"Be still, and know that I am God! I am exalted among the nations, I am exalted in the earth." PSALM 46:10

The Lord of Hosts Is Our Refuge

PSALM 46

1*God is our refuge and strength,*
a very present help in trouble.
2*Therefore we will not fear, though the earth should change,*
though the mountains shake in the heart of the sea;
3*though its waters roar and foam,*
though the mountains tremble with its tumult. Selah

4*There is a river whose streams make glad the city of God,*
the holy habitation of the Most High.
5*God is in the midst of the city; it shall not be moved;*
God will help it when the morning dawns.
6*The nations are in an uproar, the kingdoms totter;*
he utters his voice, the earth melts.
7*The Lord of hosts is with us;*
the God of Jacob is our refuge. Selah

8*Come, behold the works of the Lord;*
see what desolations he has brought on the earth.
9*He makes wars cease to the end of the earth;*
he breaks the bow, and shatters the spear;
he burns the shields with fire.
10*"Be still, and know that I am God!*

I am exalted among the nations,
I am exalted in the earth."
11 *The Lord of hosts is with us;*
the God of Jacob is our refuge. Selah

Declaring confident trust in God, this psalm describes God's defense of his people against all cosmic and geopolitical forces. In the face of all these threats, the psalm reiterates the fundamental claim of its opening verse: "God is our refuge and strength, a very present help in trouble" (verse 1). A "refuge" is a defensive fortress, a stronghold protecting people from attack. God can be counted on to guard his people, to be their "strength" and "help" in times of trouble. This confident declaration is twice reaffirmed as the psalm's refrain: "The Lord of hosts is with us; the God of Jacob is our refuge" (verses 7, 11). The ancient titles ascribed to God reinforce confidence in God's protective presence. "Lord of hosts" describes God as the divine warrior, leading the heavenly armies against cosmic and human foes. "God of Jacob" emphasizes God's faithful relationship to Israel from the time of the earliest ancestors. This powerful and trustworthy God is present with his people as their constant refuge.

It is one thing to confess that "God is our refuge and strength," but it is quite another to resolve "therefore we will not fear" (verse 2). Stating our belief in public worship is relatively easy, but bringing ourselves to personally experience trusting security in God requires the gift of faith. Faith makes us unafraid. Caution and concern may persist, but trust prevails. The psalm dares us to believe in God as our refuge even when the ground falls out from under us.

Although the source of our protection is the presence of God, the city of Jerusalem stands as the earthly symbol of that protection. Thus, this psalm of trust is also characterized as a psalm of Zion. The holy city is a refuge for those who fear, a fortress against all dangers (verses 4–5). Jerusalem is "the city of God, the holy habitation of the Most High." The king of the universe has opted to dwell there, choosing Jerusalem to represent his reign in the world.

The psalm portrays Jerusalem as the still point framed by uproar and destruction. Seeing "the mountains shake in the heart of the sea" would be the most terrorizing threat in the ancient world. The mountains were the pillars of the earth that stabilized it over the chaotic waters. As the "waters roar and foam," so the "nations are in an uproar," and as the "mountains tremble," so the "kingdoms totter" when they encounter the voice of God (verses 3, 6). Yet, through all this tumult, the city of God "shall not be moved."

In contrast to the roaring waters, there is "a river whose streams make glad the city of God." The ancient literary image of the river flowing from the mountain of God's dwelling expresses Zion as the center of the world and source of life. Ezekiel 47 develops the image as a stream flowing from the temple to become a life-giving river for the whole land, and Revelation 22 completes the images as a river flows from God's throne through the heavenly city of God. For the psalmist, the security of Jerusalem is due solely to its chief resident: "God is in the midst of the city." God's help "when the morning dawns" expresses the salvation God brings when hope seems lost in darkness. He is the sovereign of the universe and Lord of the nations.

The final section invites the nations to witness how God will end wars throughout the earth and destroy the weapons of war (verses 8–10). War is self-defeating, bringing about the destruction of those who practice it. Considering God's exaltation among the nations of the earth, international military warfare is useless. Our trust is not in a place but in a presence. For a time, God chose Jerusalem and its temple for his dwelling. But God's dwelling in time and space is never fixed and final. Above the upheaval of the world and preparations for war, God's voice is heard: "Be still, and know that I am God!"

Reflection and discussion

- When and where do I find my still point in the midst of chaos?

- What practical difference does it make in my life to know God is our refuge?

Prayer

God our Creator, you are our refuge, our strength and help in times of trouble. Calm our fears of roaring waters and warring nations. Help us be still and know that you alone are God.

Do not be afraid when some become rich, when the wealth of their houses increases. For when they die they will carry nothing away; their wealth will not go down after them. PSALM 49:16–17

God Will Ransom My Soul from Sheol

PSALM 49

1 *Hear this, all you peoples;*
give ear, all inhabitants of the world,
2 *both low and high,*
rich and poor together.
3 *My mouth shall speak wisdom;*
the meditation of my heart shall be understanding.
4 *I will incline my ear to a proverb;*
I will solve my riddle to the music of the harp.

5 *Why should I fear in times of trouble,*
when the iniquity of my persecutors surrounds me,
6 *those who trust in their wealth*
and boast of the abundance of their riches?
7 *Truly, no ransom avails for one's life,*
there is no price one can give to God for it.
8 *For the ransom of life is costly,*
and can never suffice
9 *that one should live on forever*
and never see the grave.

10 When we look at the wise, they die;
fool and dolt perish together
and leave their wealth to others.
11 Their graves are their homes forever,
their dwelling places to all generations,
though they named lands their own.
12 Mortals cannot abide in their pomp;
they are like the animals that perish.

13 Such is the fate of the foolhardy,
the end of those who are pleased with their lot. Selah
14 Like sheep they are appointed for Sheol;
Death shall be their shepherd;
straight to the grave they descend,
and their form shall waste away;
Sheol shall be their home.
15 But God will ransom my soul from the power of Sheol,
for he will receive me. Selah

16 Do not be afraid when some become rich,
when the wealth of their houses increases.
17 For when they die they will carry nothing away;
their wealth will not go down after them.
18 Though in their lifetime they count themselves happy
—for you are praised when you do well for yourself—
19 they will go to the company of their ancestors,
who will never again see the light.
20 Mortals cannot abide in their pomp;
they are like the animals that perish.

This wisdom psalm is not a prayer addressed to God but a meditation addressed to the widest possible audience. The psalmist summons all the inhabitants of the world, low in status and high alike, offering a warning for the rich and hope for the poor (verses 1–2). He will reflect deeply with his audience on a specific but universal problem of humanity (verses

3–4). The poet will take his time with this puzzling matter, speaking with his "mouth," meditating with his "heart," listening with his "ear," and chanting words of wisdom "to the music of the harp." The "riddle" he seeks to resolve is the fact that human existence ends in death, no matter how much we try to deny it. The proverb that he ponders is the repeated refrain: "Mortals cannot abide in their pomp; they are like the animals that perish" (verses 12–20).

The psalmist begins by questioning why he should fear the wickedness of his persecutors, "those who trust in their wealth and boast of the abundance of their riches" (verse 5–6). Their malice is not in the wealth itself but in the way they orient their lives to acquire and maintain it. Riches become their ultimate security and source of their values, taking the place that God alone should have. No amount of wealth can serve as a "ransom" for one's life, no payment to God would suffice to escape death, "that one should live on forever and never see the grave" (verses 7–9).

Since graves tend to be dug to roughly the same depth, death has been called the great leveler. Even though the wealthy have named property after themselves, all their residences are provisional. Wisdom offers a stark reminder: "Their graves are their homes forever, their dwelling places to all generations" (verse 10–11). All people die, just like the animals. Only the foolhardy forget or neglect this truth. Like sheep chosen to perish, they are shepherded by death into the dark and shadowy underworld of Sheol (verses 13–14).

This lengthy discussion of inevitable death is abruptly broken by the disjunctive "but," introducing the surprising declaration that "God will ransom my soul from the power of Sheol, for he will receive me" (verse 15). The psalmist professes his confidence that God will not let death cancel the relationship with him that the faithful have in life. God is more powerful than the grave and will pay the ransom to liberate the soul from death. The psalm expresses the hope that God, not Sheol, will be the final hope of the souls who trust in him. This rare hint in the Old Testament about eternal life is confirmed in the gospels as Jesus establishes that the Son of Man came "to give his life a ransom for many" (Mark 10:45). The vague hope of the psalm is illuminated by faith in the death and resurrection of Jesus.

In the final section, the poet exhorts his hearers to be confident through the wisdom he has been given (verses 16–19). Surprisingly, the poet finds freedom from fear through the fact of death. Riches, comfort, power, and fame, like life itself, are all transitory. However wealthy people may be, if they are so foolish as to forget God and not reckon with death, they are no better than the animals that spend their lives being fattened for the slaughter.

Reflection and discussion

- Can the human fascination with wealth be a denial of death?

- How does the use of the word "ransom" in verses 7–8 contrast with its use in verse 15?

- How does reflecting on verses 16–19 challenge my present lifestyle and priorities?

Prayer

Creator God, who bestows on us every blessing, help me to use wisely all of your gifts, employing them for your greater glory. Give me gratitude for my abundance and keep me focused on your kingdom.

He alone is my rock and my salvation, my fortress; I shall not be shaken. On God rests my deliverance and my honor; my mighty rock, my refuge is in God. PSALM 62:6–7

God Alone Is the Source of My Salvation

PSALM 62

1 *For God alone my soul waits in silence;*
from him comes my salvation.
2 *He alone is my rock and my salvation,*
my fortress; I shall never be shaken.

3 *How long will you assail a person,*
will you batter your victim, all of you,
as you would a leaning wall, a tottering fence?
4 *Their only plan is to bring down a person of prominence.*
They take pleasure in falsehood;
they bless with their mouths,
but inwardly they curse. Selah

5 *For God alone my soul waits in silence,*
for my hope is from him.
6 *He alone is my rock and my salvation,*
my fortress; I shall not be shaken.
7 *On God rests my deliverance and my honor;*
my mighty rock, my refuge is in God.

8 *Trust in him at all times, O people;*
pour out your heart before him;
God is a refuge for us. Selah

9 *Those of low estate are but a breath,*
those of high estate are a delusion;
in the balances they go up;
they are together lighter than a breath.
10 *Put no confidence in extortion,*
and set no vain hopes on robbery;
if riches increase, do not set your heart on them.

11 *Once God has spoken;*
twice have I heard this:
that power belongs to God,
12 *and steadfast love belongs to you, O Lord.*
For you repay to all
according to their work.

This prayer of trust reflects the confident security that the psalmist has found in God. Yet, clearly, this is not an assurance that the poet has come to easily. He is seeking to help his listeners to lay claim to the salvation he has learned to enjoy with great effort. As the psalmist speaks, he switches the recipients of his prayer throughout, creating the poem's movement.

In the opening verses, the introspective psalmist speaks to himself (verses 1–2). The experience of God's presence has transformed his weakness into confident strength. For this reason, he is able to rest in God with an inner "silence," a stillness and quietness of soul. He is able to yield his insecurities, fears, and anxieties to God in an act of trust. He describes God as "my rock," "my salvation," and "my fortress," all images that suggest a stable, unmoving, and protective presence. Although he is addressing himself, he is encouraging his listeners to seek this same confidence.

Next, the psalmist questions his adversaries and then describes their deceptive opposition (verses 3–4). In contrast to the images of stability attributed to God, the poet suggests that he and other faithful ones are "a leaning wall, a tottering fence," nearly collapsing while being assailed and battered by opponents. In contrast to the quiet confidence in God's presence, he describes the busy agitation of those without God. Their days are filled with hostility, dishonesty, and hypocrisy, cordial on the outside but vicious in secret.

The poet then returns to his introspective monologue, repeating and expanding his initial words of quiet trust (verses 5–7). Now the quiet confidence is supported with expectant "hope" that God will set things right. In the face of his hostile foes, he trusts in God's dependability. He testifies that "my deliverance" and "my honor" depend on God, who is "my mighty rock" and "my refuge."

Now the poet exhorts his listeners with a series of imperatives (verses 8–10). Foremost, he urges them to turn to God: "Trust in him at all times, O people; pour out your heart before him." Ultimate trust cannot be placed in humans, whether of "low estate" or "high estate," for mortals are essentially weak and transitory. Neither can confidence be placed in dishonest acquisition of wealth, which can never meet our needs. Nothing human can be a source of lasting stability.

The closing verses first speak about God's character, then the psalmist addresses God directly (verses 11–12). To the one God belongs two primary attributes: power and steadfast love. These both validate the trust we can place in God. Power means that God can, and steadfast love means that God desires to "repay to all according to their work." God will vindicate righteous conduct that is guided by trust and shatter the illusions of those who trust in deceit and violence.

This psalm is particularly useful for settling our souls quietly in the presence of God. Through it we muse within ourselves, we address our foes, we speak to one another, and we pray to God. We look desperately sometimes for a source of lasting security in the midst of a world that seems to be falling apart. We realize how fragile we are, how vulnerable we are to the forces that seek to bring us down. Yet, God's presence within us transforms our weakness into confident strength, for God indeed is our rock, our fortress, our refuge, and our hope.

Reflection and discussion

- How can I relinquish my insecurities, fears, and anxieties to God?

- Why is it important to trust that God is both powerfully strong as well as faithfully loving?

- How does it feel to know that God will "repay according to each one's deeds" (Rom 2:6–8)?

Prayer

O God, my rock and my salvation, I trust in your mighty strength and your unfailing love. Help me be still in your presence, in quiet confidence that you are my lasting security in a world that seems to be falling apart.

Let the nations be glad and sing for joy, for you judge the peoples with equity and guide the nations upon earth. PSALM 67:4

Let All the Peoples Praise the Lord

PSALM 67

1 *May God be gracious to us and bless us*
and make his face to shine upon us, Selah
2 *that your way may be known upon earth,*
your saving power among all nations.
3 *Let the peoples praise you, O God;*
let all the peoples praise you.

4 *Let the nations be glad and sing for joy,*
for you judge the peoples with equity
and guide the nations upon earth. Selah
5 *Let the peoples praise you, O God;*
let all the peoples praise you.

6 *The earth has yielded its increase;*
God, our God, has blessed us.
7 *May God continue to bless us;*
let all the ends of the earth revere him.

Throughout the Old Testament, Israel is described as the uniquely privileged people of God, yet God is defined as the God of all peoples and nations. This tension is first expressed in the Lord's call to

Abraham, in which God promises, "I will make of you a great nation, and I will bless you, and make your name great, so that you will be a blessing" for all the families of the earth (Gen 12:1–3). Likewise, this double calling is also felt in the prophecy of Isaiah 40—55, proclaiming that the Lord's salvation of Israel will reveal God's reign to all the nations and lead all the ends of the earth to praise the Lord. In this psalm, too, the dynamics of God's blessings and the people's praise provide the context to explore this tension.

The psalm's opening plea for God's blessing closely echoes the benediction God gave to Aaron by which he was instructed to bless Israel: "The Lord bless you and keep you; the Lord make his face to shine upon you, and be gracious to you" (Num 6:24–25). Yet, the psalm creatively reuses the traditional Aaronic blessing to introduce a congregational prayer for a blessing of God's people that will make the Lord's way "be known upon earth" and the Lord's saving power be known "among all nations" (verses 1–2). The people pray that God's blessing of Israel may be a visible sign so that all people may come to know the one God.

Forming a frame around the psalm, the final verses, too, speak of the blessing of God's people (verses 6–7). Here, God has blessed Israel with an abundant harvest, and so the people plead for God's continuing blessings upon them. Yet, their prayer is not for themselves alone. The congregation prays that God's continuing blessings may lead "all the ends of the earth" to worship and praise the Lord. What draws other nations to revere God is not military subjugation or annexation to Israel but blessings upon God's own people. The goal is not the extension of Israel's kingdom but the extension of God's praise.

Next, a refrain pleads for the universal praise of God by all people. Forming an inner frame for the psalm, the refrain is repeated twice: "Let the peoples praise you, O God; let all the peoples praise you" (verses 3, 5). Then, at the heart of the psalm is found the basis for Israel's blessings and the praise of the nations (verse 4). This is located at the center of the poem and is the only verse with three lines. Pleading that "the nations be glad and sing for joy," the psalm declares that God reigns over all the earth. All the peoples may give God praise because the Lord judges fairly and guides the nations of the earth. God's governance and guidance of Israel leads to the understanding that God is the Lord of all.

The psalm gathers the traditional language of God's blessings of Israel—the benediction of Aaron, God's covenant promises, thanksgiving for bountiful harvests, and God's faithful shepherding of his people—and remarkably extends it inclusively to all nations. God chose Israel as his own holy and priestly people as an instrument of spreading blessings to all people. The blessings of God to Israel gain the attention of the nations, and they will see through the history of Israel the revelation of God's reign over the whole world.

Reflection and discussion

- How does this psalm help me to understand why God chose Israel to be his own people?

- How can this psalm help me to broaden the scope of my prayer?

- How might God bring blessings to my life for the sake of others?

Prayer

Let the peoples praise you, O God; let all the peoples praise you. May I give you thankful praise for all the blessings of my life. Yet, may I never receive your blessings for myself alone but in order to bless the lives of others.

May his name endure forever, his fame continue as long as the sun.
May all nations be blessed in him; may they pronounce him happy.
PSALM 72:17

The Reign of God's Anointed King

PSALM 72

1 *Give the king your justice, O God,*
and your righteousness to a king's son.
2 *May he judge your people with righteousness,*
and your poor with justice.
3 *May the mountains yield prosperity for the people,*
and the hills, in righteousness.
4 *May he defend the cause of the poor of the people,*
give deliverance to the needy,
and crush the oppressor.

5 *May he live while the sun endures,*
and as long as the moon, throughout all generations.
6 *May he be like rain that falls on the mown grass,*
like showers that water the earth.
7 *In his days may righteousness flourish*
and peace abound, until the moon is no more.

8 *May he have dominion from sea to sea,*
and from the River to the ends of the earth.
9 *May his foes bow down before him,*
and his enemies lick the dust.

10 *May the kings of Tarshish and of the isles*
render him tribute,
may the kings of Sheba and Seba
bring gifts.
11 *May all kings fall down before him,*
all nations give him service.

12 *For he delivers the needy when they call,*
the poor and those who have no helper.
13 *He has pity on the weak and the needy,*
and saves the lives of the needy.
14 *From oppression and violence he redeems their life;*
and precious is their blood in his sight.

15 *Long may he live!*
May gold of Sheba be given to him.
May prayer be made for him continually,
and blessings invoked for him all day long.
16 *May there be abundance of grain in the land;*
may it wave on the tops of the mountains;
may its fruit be like Lebanon;
and may people blossom in the cities
like the grass of the field.
17 *May his name endure forever,*
his fame continue as long as the sun.
May all nations be blessed in him;
may they pronounce him happy.

18 *Blessed be the Lord, the God of Israel,*
who alone does wondrous things.
19 *Blessed be his glorious name forever;*
may his glory fill the whole earth.
Amen and Amen.

20 *The prayers of David son of Jesse are ended.*

This royal psalm was composed to honor one of the kings in Jerusalem, perhaps at his inauguration. Yet, it is not about any particular king but is concerned about the office and vocation of the royal ruler in the lineage of David. Since it is about kingship and has a general character, it could be used repeatedly for many and various occasions. It presents in poetic form the job description of the king, who is called to be the human embodiment of God's kingdom on earth.

The psalm opens with prayerful requests to God for the king, the son of the previous king in David's line (verse 1). God is asked to give the king "your justice" and "your righteousness," making clear that these attributes are given by God rather than derived from human ability. The prayer then continues to voice more specific requests based on these two primary divine attributes, praying that the king judge God's people, especially the "poor," with these gifts of righteousness and justice (verse 2). Those who are economically deprived, falsely accused, discriminated against, unjustly attacked, or in any way marginalized must be a special concern of the king. But the just rule of the king not only has social effects but ecological results as well (verse 3). A profound relationship exists between social justice and agricultural prosperity. The king is charged with the protection of God's people: defending the poor, releasing the needy from bondage, keeping the land fertile, and defeating domestic and foreign oppressors (verse 4).

The king's rule with justice and righteousness leads to a long life for him and longevity for his dynasty (verse 5). The shining sun and moon, the rain showers on the fields, and the virtue of society are all expressions of the "peace" and wholeness (in Hebrew, *shalom*) that abound when the king rules with these divine attributes (verses 6–7).

The psalm then moves from how God's people are blessed by the just rule of the king to how he will have international impact (verses 8–11). The scope of his dominion will be worldwide, as other rulers offer tribute and bow down before him. The reason for this international honor is his care for "the needy," "the poor," and "the weak" (verses 12–14). He will be known far and wide for his attention to the least of his kingdom. Not only does he judge his people fairly, he also "delivers" the needy, "saves" the lives of the poor, and "redeems" the weak from oppression and violence. The standard by which the Israelite monarchs are judged is not their military campaigns or building projects, as in ancient Egypt, Assyria, and Babylon. Rather, they are measured by how they look after the powerless within the kingdom. The anointed king must be the deliverer, savior, and redeemer for his people.

"Long live the king," both for ancient Israel and for royal rulers today, is a prayer for the ruler's well-being and the prosperity of his realm (verses 15–16). The images of high mountains and fruitful land, flourishing people in the cities and grain in the fields, all express a kingdom blessed by God because of the faithfulness of its king. As God's representative, the effective king reflects God's character to Israel and to the world. As God promised Abraham of old, the psalm pleads that "all nations be blessed in him," that God's anointed king in Israel will be God's instrument for extending blessings to all the people of the earth (verse 17).

The model of kingship presented in this psalm is not only a goal toward which each new king could aim, it is also a prescription for failure. The prayer calls for divine rule to inhabit the reign of human rulers. No monarch in Israel's history ever lived up to the royal vocation presented here. So, out of the tension between the divine ideal and the human reality comes expectations of the future Messiah. As this psalm entered the psalter, many in Israel already understood it to be a prayer for the coming of the Anointed One who would deliver, save, and redeem God's people.

We pray this psalm in its fullness only for the heir of David's lineage who is Jesus Christ. Through him, the God made known to Israel does wondrous things and establishes the kingdom of God in the world (verses 18–20). Through Jesus, the deliverer, savior, and redeemer of God's people, we pray: "Blessed be his glorious name forever; may his glory fill the whole earth."

Reflection and discussion

- What is the standard for evaluating the reigns of Israel's kings?

- Why have no earthly kings ever fulfilled the ideal established in this psalm?

- How did this prayer for Israel's king become a prayer for the coming of the Messiah?

- What indicates to me that the ideal presented in this psalm is only fulfilled in Jesus, the King of kings?

Prayer

Lord God, your kingdom of justice and peace has come upon the earth in the reign of your Son, the King of kings. May I structure my life to serve the least in your kingdom and to do your will in the world.

SUGGESTIONS FOR FACILITATORS, GROUP SESSION 3

1. Welcome group members and ask if anyone has any announcements to make.

2. You may want to pray this prayer as a group:
Lord our God, we trust in your mighty strength and your unfailing love in times of trouble. As we listen to the words of these psalms, calm our fears, help us be still in your presence, and rest in quiet confidence that you are our only lasting security. May we give you thankful praise for all the blessings of our lives, and may we so structure our lives so as to serve the least in your kingdom and to do your will in the world. May we never receive your blessings for ourselves alone, but in order to bless the lives of others.

3. Ask one or both of the following questions:
   - Which thought from the lessons this week stands out most memorably to you?
   - What is the most important lesson you learned through your study this week?

4. Discuss lessons 7 through 12. Choose one or more of the questions for reflection and discussion from each lesson to discuss as a group. You may want to ask group members which question was most challenging or helpful to them as you review each lesson.

5. Remember that there are no definitive answers for these discussion questions. The insights of group members will add to the understanding of all. None of these questions requires an expert.

6. After talking about each lesson, instruct group members to complete lessons 13 through 18 on their own during the six days before the next group meeting. They should write out their own answers to the questions as preparation for next week's group discussion.

7. Ask the group if anyone is having any particular problems with the Bible study during the week. You may want to share advice and encouragement within the group.

8. Conclude by praying aloud together the prayer at the end of one of the lessons discussed. You may add to the prayer based on the sharing that has occurred in the group.

Your people will offer themselves willingly on the day you lead your forces on the holy mountains. From the womb of the morning, like dew, your youth will come to you. PSALM 110:3

God's Priestly King Rules over the Nations

PSALM 110

1 *The Lord says to my lord,*
"Sit at my right hand
until I make your enemies your footstool."

2 *The Lord sends out from Zion*
your mighty scepter.
Rule in the midst of your foes.
3 *Your people will offer themselves willingly*
on the day you lead your forces
on the holy mountains.
From the womb of the morning,
like dew, your youth will come to you.
4 *The Lord has sworn and will not change his mind,*
"You are a priest forever according to the order of Melchizedek."

5 *The Lord is at your right hand;*
he will shatter kings on the day of his wrath.
6 *He will execute judgment among the nations,*
filling them with corpses;
he will shatter heads
over the wide earth.

[7]*He will drink from the stream by the path;*
therefore he will lift up his head.

This royal psalm was sung in association with the enthronement of the king in Jerusalem. The prophetic speaker solemnly utters two divine pronouncements (set off by quotation marks), installing the heir of King David as king and priest (verses 1, 4). Each declaration is followed by a vivid description of God as a divine warrior establishing the worldwide dominion of his chosen king.

The psalm opens with the wording commonly used to introduce divine oracles in the prophetic writings: "The Lord says." The recipient of the divine words, "my lord," is the king. The divine pronouncement "Sit at my right hand until I make your enemies your footstool" calls the king to the seat of honor at the right side of God's own throne. The king reigns secure while God subdues all the king's enemies and places them at his feet. Because the king now shares in God's worldwide dominion, his sovereignty will extend outwardly from Zion and he will rule in the midst of his enemies (verse 2).

The next verse is particularly difficult to translate from the Hebrew text (verse 3). The present version suggests that the king's forces willingly offer themselves in battle. As the dew descends at dawn upon the holy mountains, so the youth of the realm will come to fight with overwhelming abundance and might. A different interpretation of this text reads thus: "From the womb, before the dawn, I have begotten you." This version suggests that the king is God's begotten son. Both readings of the text establish the king's reign in the mighty deeds of God, who both chooses and maintains Israel's king.

The second divine declaration is also introduced with words typical of a prophetic oracle: "The Lord has sworn." The irrevocable divine oath, "You are a priest forever according to the order of Melchizedek," invests the king with the office of priest. Melchizedek is the king of ancient Salem (the earlier name of Jerusalem) and "priest of God Most High," who offered a thanksgiving sacrifice of bread and wine and blessed Abram (Gen 14:18–20). Into this royal priesthood the kings of Jerusalem are ordained and thus, as both king and priest, they draw near to God on behalf of their people.

This second oracle is again followed with a description of God as a divine warrior, establishing the worldwide dominion of his chosen king (verses 5–7). Reversing the opening image, God is now at the king's "right hand," describing his position as the king's most reliable and trusted fighter. God "will shatter kings on the day of his wrath" and "will execute judgment among the nations." Divine wrath is the justifiable anger of God at human sinfulness and God's righteous judgment. The psalm ends in striking contrast to the images of carnage and death, depicting the king drawing refreshment from a flowing brook. "The stream by the path" is the Gihon Spring, the primary water source for the city of Jerusalem and the location of the anointing ritual of the new king (1 Kings 1:38–40). The closing illustrates the complete and final victory of God and his king.

As the historical kingship of Israel waned, these two divine declarations were increasingly understood to be expressions of the prerogatives God offers to the coming Messiah. The militaristic language was progressively recognized as symbolic and visionary expressions of God's conquest of the powers of evil. Through the future messianic king and high priest, God will reign as sovereign over the kings and nations of the world.

These two divine oracles are quoted in the New Testament in reference to Jesus more than any other verses in the Psalms. Although the birth, life, passion, and death of the Messiah are in the past, Jesus Christ continues in the present to reign at the right hand of the Father, with all the powers of the world in subjection. At the same time, he continues to function as the priest of the new covenant, offering himself and the whole world as the living sacrifice to the Father.

Reflection and discussion

- What does it mean to designate Jesus Christ as both the king and priest of the kingdom of God?

- How can I prayerfully interpret the militant and violent language of the psalm?

- In what way is the ministry of Jesus Christ foreshadowed in the person of Melchizedek of old (Gen 14:18–20; Heb 7:15–19)?

- How does Jesus use this psalm to assert his own authority as the Messiah (Luke 20:41-44)?

Prayer

Most High God, you have anointed your king on Zion with royal and priestly power. I acclaim your wondrous victory over the powers of sin and death, and I give you thanks for your saving will manifested in your new covenant.

He has shown his people the power of his works, in giving them the heritage of the nations. The works of his hands are faithful and just; all his precepts are trustworthy.

PSALM 111:6–7

The Blessings of Those Who Fear the Lord

PSALM 111

1 *Praise the Lord!*
I will give thanks to the Lord with my whole heart,
in the company of the upright, in the congregation.
2 *Great are the works of the Lord,*
studied by all who delight in them.
3 *Full of honor and majesty is his work,*
and his righteousness endures forever.
4 *He has gained renown by his wonderful deeds;*
the Lord is gracious and merciful.
5 *He provides food for those who fear him;*
he is ever mindful of his covenant.
6 *He has shown his people the power of his works,*
in giving them the heritage of the nations.
7 *The works of his hands are faithful and just;*
all his precepts are trustworthy.
8 *They are established forever and ever,*
to be performed with faithfulness and uprightness.
9 *He sent redemption to his people;*
he has commanded his covenant forever.

Holy and awesome is his name.
10 *The fear of the Lord is the beginning of wisdom;*
all those who practice it have a good understanding.
His praise endures forever.

PSALM 112

1 *Praise the Lord!*
Happy are those who fear the Lord,
who greatly delight in his commandments.
2 *Their descendants will be mighty in the land;*
the generation of the upright will be blessed.
3 *Wealth and riches are in their houses,*
and their righteousness endures forever.
4 *They rise in the darkness as a light for the upright;*
they are gracious, merciful, and righteous.
5 *It is well with those who deal generously and lend,*
who conduct their affairs with justice.
6 *For the righteous will never be moved;*
they will be remembered forever.
7 *They are not afraid of evil tidings;*
their hearts are firm, secure in the Lord.
8 *Their hearts are steady, they will not be afraid;*
in the end they will look in triumph on their foes.
9 *They have distributed freely, they have given to the poor;*
their righteousness endures forever;
their horn is exalted in honor.
10 *The wicked see it and are angry;*
they gnash their teeth and melt away;
the desire of the wicked comes to nothing.

Psalms 111 and 112 begin a series that are called Alleluia psalms, all of which include the words "Praise the Lord!" These two psalms belong together, corresponding with each other in form and language. Their external form is set by the twenty-two letters of the Hebrew alphabet. The first words of each measure begin with the consecutive letters of the alphabet, providing a sense of completeness to each of these "twin" psalms. In addition, the language of these two psalms is complementary: Psalm 111 offers praise of the Lord's works by those who fear him; Psalm 112 describes the life of those who fear the Lord. Together they demonstrate that the works of God shape the lives of the righteous.

Introduced by the acclamation "Praise the Lord," Psalm 111 opens with the psalmist's stated intent to offer wholehearted thanks to God in company with the congregation (111:1). The psalm goes on to extol "the works of the Lord," which are "studied by all who delight in them" (111:2). As God's great works are reviewed and pondered by their beneficiaries, they elicit not a sense of obligation and debt but of joy and appreciation.

God's majestic works and wonderful deeds are expressions of Israel's foundational story, beginning with their liberation from Egypt and establishment in the land (111:3–9). "Gracious and merciful" are attributes of God's self-revelation after Israel's worship of the golden calf (Exodus 34:6). The provision of "food for those who fear him" recalls the gift of manna in the wilderness. God's mindfulness of the covenant evokes the promises of continuing life with God in the land. "The heritage of the nations" refers to Israel's settlement in the land. "His precepts," as they are expressed in the commandments, are also divine gifts, no less than the other saving acts. These works of God invite participation and generous response. As God's works are "faithful and just," they call forth a life of "faithfulness and uprightness." In this way, the works of the Lord are to become the works of his people.

The final verse of Psalm 111 and the first verse of Psalm 112 form the hinge that joins these psalms as a diptych. "The fear of the Lord is the beginning of wisdom" (111:10) is a saying found also in Proverbs and Job. It recommends not trepidation and dread but rather the practice of awe and reverence in the presence of God. "Happy are those who fear the Lord" begins a thorough description of the life of those who fear the Lord and delight in his commandments (112:1). "Fear" and "delight" might seem incompatible, yet they express a balanced response to studying and practicing God's way of life.

The body of this paired psalm lists God's blessings for those who fear the Lord and delight in his commandments. Their descendants will be mighty, upright, and blessed, and their houses will be filled with wealth and riches (112:2–3). As the previous psalm declared that God's "righteousness endures forever" and "the Lord is gracious and merciful," so now these same qualities describe the character of those whose lives are shaped by the Lord (112:4, 9). As God is always bounteous, so those who practice God's way of life are generous and lend to others, conducting their business with justice (112:5). As the Lord has "gained renown by his wonderful deeds," those who fear the Lord are "remembered forever" by their descendants (112:6). As God's ways are always faithful and trustworthy, so the hearts of his people are "secure in the Lord," with no reason to be afraid (112:7–8). Because their lives are shaped by God's generosity, they give freely to those in need and experience victory over their foes (112:9).

In conclusion, the happiness of those who fear the Lord is dramatically contrasted with the lives of the wicked (112:10). Their days are not filled with delight but with anger and the gnashing of teeth. Their lives form no lasting memorial but quickly come to nothing. This wise summary of who God is and how life is shaped by God's words and deeds describes the life of faith. Through a rich intertwining of language and images, these two psalms show how persons of faith partner with God to achieve a noble life full of blessings.

Reflection and discussion

- How do these twin psalms show that the works of the Lord shape the lives of those who fear the Lord?

- How do I want my life to be "remembered forever," to be a memorial for my descendants?

Prayer

Lord God, a fearful reverence of you leads me to a life of wisdom. Let me always look to the faithfulness and justice of your ways, so that I may be formed in your covenant and become a light in the darkness for others.

From the rising of the sun to its setting the name of the Lord is to be praised. The Lord is high above all nations, and his glory above the heavens. PSALM 113:3–4

Praise for the Majesty and Mercy of the Lord

PSALM 113

1 *Praise the Lord!*
Praise, O servants of the Lord;
praise the name of the Lord.

2 *Blessed be the name of the Lord*
from this time on and forevermore.
3 *From the rising of the sun to its setting*
the name of the Lord is to be praised.
4 *The Lord is high above all nations,*
and his glory above the heavens.

5 *Who is like the Lord our God,*
who is seated on high,
6 *who looks far down*
on the heavens and the earth?
7 *He raises the poor from the dust,*
and lifts the needy from the ash heap,
8 *to make them sit with princes,*
with the princes of his people.
9 *He gives the barren woman a home,*
making her the joyous mother of children.
Praise the Lord!

PSALM 114

1 *When Israel went out from Egypt,*
the house of Jacob from a people of strange language,
2 *Judah became God's sanctuary,*
Israel his dominion.

3 *The sea looked and fled;*
Jordan turned back.
4 *The mountains skipped like rams,*
the hills like lambs.

5 *Why is it, O sea, that you flee?*
O Jordan, that you turn back?
6 *O mountains, that you skip like rams?*
O hills, like lambs?

7 *Tremble, O earth, at the presence of the Lord,*
at the presence of the God of Jacob,
8 *who turns the rock into a pool of water,*
the flint into a spring of water.

The invitation to praise the Lord is offered to the "servants of the Lord," all those claimed by God as his own. The "name of the Lord" is the mode of God's presence within the worshipping congregation, bearing the identity of a God who cannot be imagined or encountered by the senses. Such praise of God is everlasting and universal, unlimited by time or space (113:1–3). Yet, the Lord is not only transcendent but also immanent, both majestic and merciful.

This great God is incomparable, high above the nations and glorious above the heavens. Although reigning over and beyond every sphere of power, he is concerned about the earth below (113:4–6). Making himself both high and low, the Lord can be depicted as both the victorious warrior and the gentle shepherd, the mighty king and the tender father. Two illustrations indicate how God acts with compassion upon the helpless (113:7–9). The poor and needy are raised up and seated with the elite, and the barren woman is made the joyous mother of children. The Torah and prophets contain numerous examples of how the Lord intervenes to cause extreme reversals in the circumstances of his people.

Psalm 114 describes how the Lord of heaven and earth came to dwell in the midst of Israel, freeing them from their oppressors and making them his own (114:1–2). It poetically describes the tumult of nature as it experiences God's presence: the sea and river retreated; the mountains and hills leapt like startled sheep (114:3–6). The earth is called to "tremble" at the Lord's presence, each natural element acting beyond its own nature on behalf of God's own people (114:7–8). The massive waters hold back, the immovable mountains skip, and the hard rock produces a living spring of water for a thirsty people.

These two psalms begin a cycle of six hymns that found a special place in the liturgy of Israel's Passover. Psalms 113 to 118 are called the Hallel psalms in the Jewish tradition, and the gospels indicate that this collection of psalms was sung by Jesus and his disciples at the Last Supper (Mark 14:26). The two redeeming events—the receding of the sea as Israel escaped the pursuing Egyptians and the turning back of the Jordan River as Israel entered the promised land—form the twin poles of the exodus event. Between these events are the giving of the covenant at Mount Sinai, the wandering in the wilderness, and the miraculous feeding of the people's hunger and the quenching of their thirst.

Psalm 114 is a perfect example of the parallelism of Hebrew poetry, as every two lines correspond to each other. Egypt and "people of strange language," sanctuary and dominion, mountains and hills, rams and lambs, sea and river, pool and spring—these matching lines have the effect of slowing down the chanting of the psalm, causing us to go over everything twice, prolonging our prayer and deepening our meditation.

Reflection and discussion

- What is another scene of Scripture that illustrates both the majesty and mercy of God?

- What indicates to me that God continues to cause extreme reversals in the circumstances of his people?

- What do each of the wondrous events of Psalm 114 have in common?

Prayer

Holy One of Israel, who looks far down on the heavens and the earth, may we praise your name forevermore. As you raise the poor from their gloom and the barren from their desperation, come to the aid of your people and redeem us from our sin.

May the Lord give you increase, both you and your children.
May you be blessed by the Lord, who made heaven and earth.
PSALM 115:14–15

Praise to Our Free and Faithful God

PSALM 115

1 *Not to us, O Lord, not to us, but to your name give glory,*
for the sake of your steadfast love and your faithfulness.
2 *Why should the nations say,*
"Where is their God?"

3 *Our God is in the heavens;*
he does whatever he pleases.
4 *Their idols are silver and gold,*
the work of human hands.
5 *They have mouths, but do not speak;*
eyes, but do not see.
6 *They have ears, but do not hear;*
noses, but do not smell.
7 *They have hands, but do not feel;*
feet, but do not walk;
they make no sound in their throats.
8 *Those who make them are like them;*
so are all who trust in them.

9 *O Israel, trust in the Lord!*
He is their help and their shield.

10O house of Aaron, trust in the Lord!
He is their help and their shield.
11You who fear the Lord, trust in the Lord!
He is their help and their shield.

12The Lord has been mindful of us; he will bless us;
he will bless the house of Israel;
he will bless the house of Aaron;
13he will bless those who fear the Lord,
both small and great.

14May the Lord give you increase,
both you and your children.
15May you be blessed by the Lord,
who made heaven and earth.

16The heavens are the Lord's heavens,
but the earth he has given to human beings.
17The dead do not praise the Lord,
nor do any that go down into silence.
18But we will bless the Lord
from this time on and forevermore.
Praise the Lord!

The psalm offers praise to the Lord, satirically contrasting "our God" and "their idols." The variation of speakers, addressees, and references—us and we, you and your, and third-person references—implies that the psalm was performed liturgically, not simply proclaimed by one person. Different voices chanted different sections, and some verses were sung antiphonally.

Other nations of the ancient world measured the success of their gods by the nation's political and military success. The Lord of Israel is glorified for the sake of his steadfast love and faithfulness. Although the nations ask, "Where is their God?" chiding Israel for God's seeming absence in their need, the people of Israel express confidence: "Our God is in the heavens; he does whatever he pleases" (verses 1–3). This testifies to the Lord's absolute freedom, transcending the affairs of nations and unable to be manipulated by earthly influences and human controls.

In contrast, the gods of other nations are mere idols (verses 4–8). In stark contrast to the Lord, these idols are totally ineffective. Crafted by human hands from precious but ineffective metals, they are crafted to look like those who worship them. Although they have mouths, eyes, ears, noses, hands, and feet, they are utterly senseless and idle. Those who make these idols and those who trust in them "are like them," mindless and useless. Humans become like what they worship: revering idols, they become lifeless; praising God, they are transformed into his likeness.

Those who "trust in the Lord" receive his support and protection: "He is their help and their shield" (verses 9–11). When the verses are sung alternately, God's people express their confidence in the Lord. Because God has always been mindful of his people, remembering them in their need, they know that he will bless them now. God will send his blessings upon all those who hold him in reverential fear, whether they are small or great, poor or powerful (verses 12–13). God will send blessings, not just in the momentous deliverances of the nation but in the daily blessings of individuals and families (verse 14–15). The maker of heaven and earth will surely bless those who trust in his steadfast love and faithfulness.

The heavens are the realm that God governs, but the earth is God's gift to human beings (verse 16). From the Lord's sovereignty, he has willed that man and woman be responsible stewards of the earth. The psalm summons God's people to live by the knowledge of God given to them throughout their history. The one who has always been their help and their shield will continue to bless them. They must live by this promise and be sustained by it in the midst of the nations. And as God blesses his people, they will bless their God: "We will bless the Lord from this time on and forevermore" (verse 18).

Reflection and discussion

- Why does the Torah forbid creating visible images of the Lord?

- Why does the psalm encourage God's people to aspire to virtues like "trust" and "fear" rather than power and success?

- What are some of the idols people have today? In what sense do we become like what we worship?

Prayer

Maker of heaven and earth, you share your life with the people you have called to be your own. Help me to trust in you as my help and shield, and transform me to reflect your image in the world.

I will lift up the cup of salvation and call on the name of the Lord,
I will pay my vows to the Lord in the presence of all his people.
PSALM 116:13–14

A Thanksgiving Sacrifice to the Lord

PSALM 116

1 *I love the Lord, because he has heard*
my voice and my supplications.
2 *Because he inclined his ear to me,*
therefore I will call on him as long as I live.
3 *The snares of death encompassed me;*
the pangs of Sheol laid hold on me;
I suffered distress and anguish.
4 *Then I called on the name of the Lord:*
"O Lord, I pray, save my life!"

5 *Gracious is the Lord, and righteous;*
our God is merciful.
6 *The Lord protects the simple;*
when I was brought low, he saved me.
7 *Return, O my soul, to your rest,*
for the Lord has dealt bountifully with you.

8 *For you have delivered my soul from death,*
my eyes from tears,
my feet from stumbling.
9 *I walk before the Lord*
in the land of the living.

[10]*I kept my faith, even when I said,*
"I am greatly afflicted";
[11]*I said in my consternation,*
"Everyone is a liar."

[12]*What shall I return to the Lord*
for all his bounty to me?
[13]*I will lift up the cup of salvation*
and call on the name of the Lord,
[14]*I will pay my vows to the Lord*
in the presence of all his people.
[15]*Precious in the sight of the Lord*
is the death of his faithful ones.
[16]*O Lord, I am your servant;*
I am your servant, the child of your serving girl.
You have loosed my bonds.
[17]*I will offer to you a thanksgiving sacrifice*
and call on the name of the Lord.
[18]*I will pay my vows to the Lord*
in the presence of all his people,
[19]*in the courts of the house of the Lord,*
in your midst, O Jerusalem.
Praise the Lord!

This psalm of thanksgiving joyfully testifies to God's rescue in a time of trouble. The opening assertion, "I love the Lord," defines the whole song as a declaration of grateful love for God. The Lord has "inclined his ear" and heard the psalmist's voice when he pleaded for help (verses 1–2). His witness assures others that prayers do indeed move God to act on our behalf and that they can always call upon him in their times of affliction.

The "snares of death" and the "pangs of Sheol" may refer to a deadly illness or injury, but they could just as well express the trauma caused by slander or the distress brought on by persecutors and enemies (verse 3). The psalmist's cry, "O Lord, I pray, save my life!" pleads for rescue from numerous physical, mental, or spiritual traumas (verse 4). He is intentionally vague when speaking about his former distress, not intending to describe what happened but to testify to the Lord's gracious and merciful help: "When I was brought low, he saved me" (verses 5–6). Even when greatly afflicted and when it seemed "everyone is a liar," God delivered his soul from death, his eyes from tears, and his feet from stumbling, so that he could continue to stand and walk in the way of the Lord (verses 7–11).

The final section of the psalm, introduced by the question "What shall I return to the Lord for all his bounty to me?" is a pledge to present a liturgical offering in gratitude to God (verse 12). Thanksgiving to God is more than an inner feeling; it is a ritualized response performed in the presence of others. Although God's goodness can never be repaid, the Israelites traditionally vowed to offer a thanksgiving sacrifice after rescue from serious harm (see Lev 7:11–15). This included the sacrifice of a lamb and the sharing of the sacrifice in the form of a sacred meal, including bread and wine. The psalm is full of liturgical language and actions: lifting the cup of salvation, calling on the Lord's name, and paying vows to the Lord in the courts of the temple in Jerusalem (verses 13–19).

Although this offering was usually made by an individual rescued by God, the Passover was the communal thanksgiving sacrifice of God's people. This psalm is one of the Hallel psalms sung at the sacrificial Passover meal in connection with the fourth cup. For Christians, the psalm is associated with the Last Supper and the Eucharist, fulfilling the thanksgiving sacrifices of the original covenant and remembering the ultimate redemption found in Jesus Christ.

Reflection and discussion

- Why does one who is rescued by God from deadly harm express thanksgiving in song and ritual?

- What elements of this psalm associate it with the Jewish Passover and the Christian Eucharist?

- Why is the psalmist's trauma described in such general terms? When has God rescued me from such serious distress?

- What do I experience as I pray this psalm as thanksgiving to God for salvation from the threat of sin and final death?

Prayer

Lord God, I call upon your name and give you thanks for your goodness to me. You have delivered my soul from death, my eyes from tears, and my feet from stumbling, so I may walk always with you in the land of the living.

The Lord is your keeper; the Lord is your shade at your right hand. The sun shall not strike you by day, nor the moon by night.

PSALM 121:5–6

The Lord Will Keep You from Harm

PSALM 121

1 *I lift up my eyes to the hills—*
from where will my help come?
2 *My help comes from the Lord,*
who made heaven and earth.

3 *He will not let your foot be moved;*
he who keeps you will not slumber.
4 *He who keeps Israel*
will neither slumber nor sleep.

5 *The Lord is your keeper;*
the Lord is your shade at your right hand.
6 *The sun shall not strike you by day,*
nor the moon by night.

7 *The Lord will keep you from all evil;*
he will keep your life.
8 *The Lord will keep*
your going out and your coming in
from this time on and forevermore.

This is a prayer for safe travel. It instills a sense of trust in God's presence and protection that can sustain travelers, whether they are on a pilgrimage to Jerusalem or on the journey of life. When setting out, the travelers survey the horizon to find the right direction. The first stanza is held together by the repetition of "my help" in the question and answer: "From where will my help come? My help comes from the Lord" (verses 1–2).

As travelers looks toward "the hills," they might sense the ambiguity in the question. Are these hills a help or hindrance for the journey? Do the hills provide protection for those journeying on foot to their destination, or do they protect would-be attackers who often hide in them? Does the question concerning from where help comes contrast the many "high places" where the temples of various gods are found with the one holy hill where the Lord is worshipped in Jerusalem? Regardless of the emphasis placed on the question's many meanings, the answer leaves no doubt about the ultimate source of help for all travelers. "The Lord who made heaven and earth" is the protective guard for all on the journey.

The theme of God's help on the journey is expressed repeatedly in the remaining stanza through the verbal idea of "keep," repeated six times in different forms. God is the "keeper" of his people, the one who "keeps" them from harm, guarding and protecting them along the way (verses 3, 4, 5, 7, 8).

Traveling was dangerous in the ancient world. The traveler could fall off one of the high, narrow mountain paths; the traveler could suffer heatstroke from the sun or be attacked by the many robbers that often assaulted those on the road. Yet, the psalm praises God's safekeeping care. God "will not let your foot be moved," and his protection is constant. The Lord "who keeps Israel" is ever attentive; like a vigilant watchman he will neither "slumber nor sleep." Although the sun and moon were often worshipped by the peoples surrounding Israel, only the Lord overshadows his people, protecting them by day and by night.

Despite the challenges of travel and the difficulties of the journey, God's people hold a deep conviction that the whole of life is safe in God's keeping. Travel reminds us that we are always in God's hands, and this prayer for safe travel reminds us that we can trust the Lord to guard us on our way. The psalm professes the all-inclusiveness of God's protective presence: "The Lord will keep you from all evil," in every place; "The Lord will keep your going out and your coming in," and always, "from this time on and forevermore" (verse 7–8).

This psalm was adopted as one of Israel's "Songs of Ascents" (Pss 120 to 134), a collection of psalms sung by pilgrims as they traveled up to Jerusalem for the pilgrim feasts. Israelites from many different lands would make the long, dangerous journey. From whatever direction the pilgrims came, the way to Jerusalem was always upward. Yet, the journey was one not only of geographical ascent but also a spiritual ascent of the mind and heart to the house of God. Every sacred journey remembered the first journey of God's people, the perilous way through the wilderness, the journey from the bondage of slavery to the land flowing with milk and honey. Going on pilgrimage is a way of teaching us how to live, how to understand our whole life as pilgrimage toward the goal of life in its fullness.

Reflection and discussion

- When have I been on a journey that required trust? When did I feel most vulnerable? What helped me experience God's protection?

- In what way does religious pilgrimage help me understand the journey of life as a pilgrimage toward God?

Prayer

Lord of heaven and earth, I place my trust in you in all my coming and going. Be my guard by day and my watchman at night. Protect me from all evil and shelter me with your watchful care, now and forever.

SUGGESTIONS FOR FACILITATORS, GROUP SESSION 4

1. Welcome group members and ask if anyone has any questions, announcements, or requests.

2. You may want to pray this prayer as a group:
Maker of heaven and earth, you share your life with the people you have called to be your own, and you teach us to trust in you in all our coming and going. As you have delivered our souls from death, our eyes from tears, and our feet from stumbling, so may we walk always with you in the land of the living. Protect us from all evil, and shelter us with your watchful care. Be our guard by day and our watchman at night as we call upon your name now and forevermore.

3. Ask one or both of the following questions:
   - What is the most difficult part of this study for you?
   - What insights stand out for you from the lessons this week?

4. Discuss lessons 13 through 18. Choose one or more of the questions for reflection and discussion from each lesson to discuss as a group. You may want to ask group members which question was most challenging or helpful for them as you review each lesson.

5. Keep the discussion moving but allow time for the questions that provoke the most discussion. Encourage the group members to use "I" language in their responses.

6. After talking over each lesson, instruct group members to complete lessons 19 through 24 on their own during the six days before the next group meeting. They should write out their own answers to the questions as preparation for next week's session.

7. Ask the group what encouragement they need for the coming week. Ask the members to pray for the needs of one another during the week.

8. Conclude by praying aloud together the prayer at the end of one of the lessons discussed. You may choose to conclude the prayer by asking members to pray aloud any requests they may have.

Pray for the peace of Jerusalem: "May they prosper who love you. Peace be within your walls, and security within your towers."
PSALM 122:6–7

Up to the House of the Lord

PSALM 122

1 *I was glad when they said to me,*
"Let us go to the house of the Lord!"
2 *Our feet are standing*
within your gates, O Jerusalem.

3 *Jerusalem—built as a city*
that is bound firmly together.
4 *To it the tribes go up,*
the tribes of the Lord,
as was decreed for Israel,
to give thanks to the name of the Lord.
5 *For there the thrones for judgment were set up,*
the thrones of the house of David.

6 *Pray for the peace of Jerusalem:*
"May they prosper who love you.
7 *Peace be within your walls,*
and security within your towers."
8 *For the sake of my relatives and friends*
I will say, "Peace be within you."

9 *For the sake of the house of the Lord our God,*
I will seek your good.

This pilgrimage psalm opens with an expression of delight that permeates the entire work. Jerusalem as the site of "the house of the Lord" frames the psalm, as stated in the first and last verses. The psalm overflows with joy over the holy city in each of its three stanzas: being present within its gates, contemplating its central place in Israel's life, and praying for its peace.

The psalmist is clearly not alone on pilgrimage. As the travelers set foot within the city of Jerusalem, they each remember the gladness they felt as they were invited to make a pilgrimage to the house of the Lord (verses 1–2). The anticipation, the journey, and the arrival fill the travelers with joy as they await the spatial and liturgical experience of nearness to the Lord's presence in his temple.

The second stanza offers praise for the distinctive qualities of Jerusalem. As a city that is "bound firmly together," it serves as a place of safety and defense (verse 3). The city stands secure against hostile powers, its walls and towers expressing the refuge it offers to those who trust in the Lord. There "the tribes go up" on pilgrimage, as was prescribed by God in the Torah (verse 4). There is no division in Israel's literature between the duties imposed by the law and the joy of living those prescriptions as God's people. On the fixed feasts of Israel, the twelve tribes travel from throughout the land and meet in their capital city "to give thanks to the name of the Lord." In addition to being a city of refuge and pilgrimage, it is the place where justice is established. The "thrones for judgment" are the legal institutions set up under the monarchy of David (verse 5). Conflicts that went unsettled in the local courts were brought to the royal officials in Jerusalem.

In the third stanza, the psalmist invites the community of pilgrims to "pray for the peace of Jerusalem" (verses 6–9). The prayer expresses what "peace" (in Hebrew, *shalom*) involves for the holy city. Certainly, this peace implies tranquility that is undisturbed by social conflicts within and dread of enemies without. It concerns "relatives and friends" who seek an agreeable balance they have lost in daily life. The prayer for Jerusalem, "Peace be within you," invokes well-being for the city, without which God cannot fulfill the divine purposes for the place of his dwelling.

Yet, this city that brings joy to pilgrims is also the landscape over which Jesus wept, "the city that kills the prophets and stones those who are sent to it!" (Matt 23:37). Of its walls and towers, "not one stone will be left here upon another; all will be thrown down" (Matt 24:2). Tears of lament reveal how deeply Jesus cared for this city and shared the psalm's concern for the peace of Jerusalem: "If you, even you, had only recognized on this day the things that make for peace!" (Luke 19:42). Although we continue to pray today for the peace of Jerusalem, which is divided and weary with war, we also anticipate "the new Jerusalem, coming down out of heaven from God" to a renewed earth (Rev 21:2). For this we also pray.

Reflection and discussion

- What is the emotional response of God's people toward fulfilling their religious responsibilities? Do I feel the same way about my religious duties?

- What are some of the elements that would make Jerusalem live up to its name: the city of peace?

- In what ways do I share the love, grief, and hopes of Jesus for Jerusalem?

Prayer

Ever-living God, as we look to the day when Jerusalem will be truly a city of peace where all will dwell free from conflicts and dread, may the joy of your peace abide in our hearts and radiate to our relatives and friends.

As the eyes of servants look to the hand of their master, as the eyes of a maid to the hand of her mistress, so our eyes look to the Lord our God, until he has mercy upon us. PSALM 123:2–3

Our Help Is in the Name of the Lord

PSALM 123

1 *To you I lift up my eyes,*
O you who are enthroned in the heavens!
2 *As the eyes of servants*
look to the hand of their master,
as the eyes of a maid
to the hand of her mistress,
so our eyes look to the Lord our God,
until he has mercy upon us.

3 *Have mercy upon us, O Lord, have mercy upon us,*
for we have had more than enough of contempt.
4 *Our soul has had more than its fill*
of the scorn of those who are at ease,
of the contempt of the proud.

PSALM 124

1 *If it had not been the Lord who was on our side*
—let Israel now say—
2 *if it had not been the Lord who was on our side,*
when our enemies attacked us,

3 *then they would have swallowed us up alive,*
when their anger was kindled against us;
4 *then the flood would have swept us away,*
the torrent would have gone over us;
5 *then over us would have gone*
the raging waters.

6 *Blessed be the Lord,*
who has not given us
as prey to their teeth.
7 *We have escaped like a bird*
from the snare of the fowlers;
the snare is broken,
and we have escaped.

8 *Our help is in the name of the Lord,*
who made heaven and earth.

Eyes are a compelling indicator of a person's emotional or spiritual outlook. We speak with our eyes. We can read the eyes as they indicate the intentions of another. Eyes bright with joy, eyes welling with tears, eyes eager for an answer, and eyes grateful for a response—all convey the inner state of the other. We encounter the word "eyes" four times in the opening two verses of Psalm 123. "To you I lift up my eyes" expresses the psalmist's hopeful expectation from God, the sovereign one "enthroned in the heavens" (123:1). As the eyes of servants or maids look to the hand of their superiors for approval or instructions, "so our eyes look to the Lord our God" (123:2).

Those praying this psalm plead for God's gracious mercy with persistent expectation (123:3–4). They look for compassionate kindness in a world that shows them only contempt and scorn. Their plea does not specify precisely what kind of help they need from the Lord. The point is only the contrast between "the contempt of the proud" and the mercy they find when they lift their eyes to behold the one who rules the world.

Psalm 124 recalls a past experience when the Lord delivered his people when they were attacked by their enemies. They acknowledge that they would not have survived without God's acting on their behalf. Trapped by the enemy, they felt helpless, yet with God's help, they escaped unharmed.

Voicing their praise to God, the people suggest that the Lord was on their side (124:1–2). The idea that God is on one side or another often offends modern sensibilities. Yet, biblical texts are filled with accounts of God being on the side of those who trust in his ways. We who look to God in every aspect of life, especially in times of trouble, must come to understand that God will go before us, that he will lead the way. The Lord is on our side in the sense that he is working on our behalf and for our good. As Paul asked, "If God is for us, who can be against us?" (Rom 8:31). When we cry out to him, God hears us and comes to our aid, determined to save us.

Again, this psalm is not specific about the kind of help God's people need from him. The point is their helplessness and God's gracious rescue. The danger of their situation is expressed with several frightening images (124:3–5). "They would have swallowed us up alive" is a thought too horrible to ponder. "The flood would have swept us away" evokes the sense of a power over which they have no control.

The recollection is not designed to tell us what happened but to dramatize how great was the danger and how narrow the escape. Like a bird that escapes the fowler's snare, God's people have survived when all seemed lost (124:7). And so, we are invited to sing confidently with the psalm's chorus, "Our help is in the name of the Lord, who made heaven and earth."

Reflection and discussion

- Why are these psalms so vague and general about the circumstances and events they recall?

- How is lifting up my eyes to God a form of prayer?

- When has God been my advocate and rescued me when the situation seemed hopeless?

- Does God take sides? In battles, in disputes, in sports matches? Why does Israel say that the Lord was on their side?

Prayer

Lord of heaven and earth, you are our advocate and help in times of distress. When we cry out to you, come to our aid and hear our prayer. To you I lift my eyes with confident trust.

Those who go out weeping, bearing the seed for sowing, shall come home with shouts of joy, carrying their sheaves. PSALM 126:6

Praying for God's Blessing

PSALM 125

1 *Those who trust in the Lord are like Mount Zion,*
which cannot be moved, but abides forever.
2 *As the mountains surround Jerusalem,*
so the Lord surrounds his people,
from this time on and forevermore.
3 *For the scepter of wickedness shall not rest*
on the land allotted to the righteous,
so that the righteous might not stretch out
their hands to do wrong.
4 *Do good, O Lord, to those who are good,*
and to those who are upright in their hearts.
5 *But those who turn aside to their own crooked ways*
the Lord will lead away with evildoers.
Peace be upon Israel!

PSALM 126

1 *When the Lord restored the fortunes of Zion,*
we were like those who dream.
2 *Then our mouth was filled with laughter,*
and our tongue with shouts of joy;
then it was said among the nations,
"The Lord has done great things for them."
3 *The Lord has done great things for us,*
and we rejoiced.

4 *Restore our fortunes, O Lord,*
like the watercourses in the Negeb.
5 *May those who sow in tears*
reap with shouts of joy.
6 *Those who go out weeping,*
bearing the seed for sowing,
shall come home with shouts of joy,
carrying their sheaves.

PSALM 127

1 *Unless the Lord builds the house,*
those who build it labor in vain.
Unless the Lord guards the city,
the guard keeps watch in vain.
2 *It is in vain that you rise up early*
and go late to rest,
eating the bread of anxious toil;
for he gives sleep to his beloved.

3 *Sons are indeed a heritage from the Lord,*
the fruit of the womb a reward.
4 *Like arrows in the hand of a warrior*
are the sons of one's youth.
5 *Happy is the man who has*
his quiver full of them.
He shall not be put to shame
when he speaks with his enemies in the gate.

These psalms continue Israel's "Songs of Ascents" (Pss 120 to 134), a collection of psalms sung by pilgrims as they traveled up to Jerusalem for its feasts. They are well suited as travel songs by their form—characterized by brevity, key words, and repetition—and by their emphasis on Zion and their sense of hopefulness. While the pilgrims longed to get to Jerusalem and its temple, they found joy along the journey and gave praise to

God in song. These Songs of Ascents reminded God's people of divine grace, mercy, provision, protection, and salvation. Their journey was one not only of geographical ascent but also of spiritual ascent of the mind and heart to God.

When pilgrims reach the point in their journey where Jerusalem comes into view, they see the city in its distinctiveness. Psalm 125 expresses this thrilling perspective: the view of Zion as a mountaintop stronghold protectively surrounded by other mountains (125:1–2). The landscape of the city encircled by mountains reminds the singers that the embracing arms of God are protecting Jerusalem and its people. This image of divine care evokes Israel's trust in God, who established Zion as the place where God would dwell with his people "from this time on and forevermore."

Yet, there follows a warning that the reign of wickedness must not be allowed to remain in the land of God's righteous ones (125:3). The examples of both the good and the wicked have a lasting impact on the lives of those with whom they live, learn, and do business. We will come to be like them, and they will become like us. The psalm concludes with a prayer that the Lord bestow blessings on those who do good and are "upright in their hearts" while leading away those who practice "crooked ways" (125:4). The desired result is that true "peace"—well-being of mind, heart, and body—may rest upon God's people.

The exodus (literally, the way out) of God's people from oppression to liberation is experienced over and over again in Israel's history. Psalm 126 expresses the wonders of God's rescue of his people from the apparent hopelessness of captivity in Babylon. As God reversed the fortunes of the people of Zion, they thought they were dreaming (126:1). Their lives were then filled with laughter and rejoicing, and they exclaimed, "The Lord has done great things for us" (126:2–3).

As God's people remember the past deliverances of God, they grow in confidence that God will continually provide the way out. So, they continue to plead, "Restore our fortunes, O Lord." The prayer offers us two images of restoration: the first is a sheer gift, like the rain that fills up the dry waterways in the wilderness of the Negeb; the second requires more time and effort—sowing tears that in time will reap sheaves of joy (126:4–6). Our very human response to suffering is the seed that God uses to bring us joy. The seeds of our sorrows, when planted in the ground of confident hope, are transformed into an abundant harvest, resulting in shouts of joyful gratitude.

Psalm 127 proclaims that the tasks of human life—building a house, guarding a city, and creating a family—are truly the Lord's work. Building a house means not only constructing an edifice but also creating a lineage. Guarding a city means not only defending the walls and towers but also protecting the life within it. Creating a family means not only having lots of children but also establishing a legacy. All of these human tasks seem to demand rising early from sleep, going to bed late, and lots of "anxious toil" (127:2). Yet, the psalm reminds the singers that none of these endeavors will come to fruition unless they are entrusted to God's loving care.

Behind all our labors in life abides the gracious unfolding of God's mysterious plan. Our home, city, and family are the arena of God's saving work. In that arena, we each have our part to play. The challenge is to find that delicate balance between trusting totally in God's grace and making good use of the gifts God has given us. As we travel the path of life with fellow pilgrims, we express our confidence in what emerges from God's grace and our efforts.

Reflection and discussion

- When have the seeds of my sorrow resulted in a harvest of joy? How did God use my suffering to bring about a situation of rejoicing?

- What does Psalm 127 teach me about how to approach the basic tasks of my life?

Prayer

Ever-living God, our ancestors in the faith have taught us to trust in your guidance through sorrow and joy. Teach me to avoid greed and restless anxiety and to place my confidence in your loving plan.

O Israel, hope in the Lord! For with the Lord there is steadfast love, and with him is great power to redeem. PSALM 130:7

Waiting and Hoping in the Lord

PSALM 130

1*Out of the depths I cry to you, O Lord.*
2*Lord, hear my voice!*
Let your ears be attentive
to the voice of my supplications!

3*If you, O Lord, should mark iniquities,*
Lord, who could stand?
4*But there is forgiveness with you,*
so that you may be revered.

5*I wait for the Lord, my soul waits,*
and in his word I hope;
6*my soul waits for the Lord*
more than those who watch for the morning,
more than those who watch for the morning.

7*O Israel, hope in the Lord!*
For with the Lord there is steadfast love,
and with him is great power to redeem.
8*It is he who will redeem Israel*
from all its iniquities.

PSALM 131

1 *O Lord, my heart is not lifted up,*
my eyes are not raised too high;
I do not occupy myself with things
too great and too marvelous for me.
2 *But I have calmed and quieted my soul,*
like a weaned child with its mother;
my soul is like the weaned child that is with me.

3 *O Israel, hope in the Lord*
from this time on and forevermore.

Psalm 130 is a succinct expression of the human predicament from which we are in need of God's saving grace. The human heart is mysteriously inclined to seek out ways that separate us from God and neighbor. Crying to God "out of the depths" means imploring the Lord while overwhelmed by turbulent waters, drowning in confusion, sucked into chaos and confusion (130:1–2). The depths are as far away from God as one can get, a distance that causes severe distress. The psalmist is making a desperate effort to draw God's attention to this plight.

The rhetorical question "If you, O Lord, should mark iniquities, Lord, who could stand?" presents an erroneous understanding of God and its consequences for the human condition (130:3). God is not one who keeps an eye out for human iniquities and keeps track of all our sins. Although we have plenty of iniquities and all people stand as sinners before God, none of us would survive if this were God's way. Instead, the psalm presents the truth about God and its significance for the human condition: "There is forgiveness with you, so that you may be revered" (130:4). From the turbulence of sin and its consequences, from which we cannot escape, we depend on God's forgiving grace to rescue us. God has both the authority and the desire to forgive our iniquities. And as we experience this forgiveness, God draws us into a reverent and trusting relationship with himself whose way is mercy.

The second half of the psalm describes the appropriate stance for those sinking in the depths of iniquity: "I wait for the Lord, my soul waits, and in his word I hope" (130:5). Waiting for the Lord with hope is the way to escape the flood of sin and be rescued by God. This hope is the result of the divine promises of God's word, a hope that will not be discouraged in the midst of struggle. So, after moving from a frantic cry from the depths, a desperate plea for God to listen, the psalm rests in a gentle image of waiting for the Lord, like "those who watch for the morning" (130:6). This lovely phrase is repeated a second time as the poet contemplates the scene of waiting at dawn in confident trust.

The psalmist's experience has embodied both the iniquity and the hope of Israel. In its closing verses, the psalm urges the congregation to "hope in the Lord" (130:7–8). This stance before God provides courage and strength, rooted in the certainty of what is yet to be. All must wait in hope, trusting that they will experience God's forgiveness, faithful love, and merciful redemption.

The hopeful waiting and restful anticipation expressed in Psalm 130 provides an apt segue into the deeply moving expression of contentment in Psalm 131. The psalmist disavows the self-centered pride and ambition that can arise with a failure to trust in God (131:1). Instead, he expresses a sober self-awareness that shuns the pursuit of those things that are "too great and too marvelous." Such confidence comes from a clear vision of the incomparable magnitude and tender mercy of God.

Such humble contentment is expressed by the poet in the striking image of the "weaned child with its mother" (131:2). The child that has passed through the stage of grasping at its mother's breast now rests contentedly in its mother's arms with no other need than the security of her calming and comforting presence. The soul of the psalmist is like this trusting child, quietly and confidently resting in God.

The psalm's conclusion extends the call of the previous psalm, "O Israel, hope in the Lord" (130:7; 131:3). Psalm 130 has brought the congregation to a stance of confident hope in God's promises, and Psalm 131 expresses the secure tranquility that results from such hope. The abstract idea of "hope in the Lord" is beautifully conveyed in the poignant picture of the child and its mother.

Reflection and discussion

- What is the erroneous understanding of God's ways in Psalm 130:3? How does it contrast with the true understanding of God's ways in Psalm 130:4? What are the consequences of these contrasting ways for my life?

- How can I move from a frantic crying "out of the depths" to a confident hope in God's word?

- It has been said that Psalm 131 is one of the shortest psalms to read but one of the longest to learn. Do I find this to be so?

Prayer

God of unfailing love, hear my plea for help. Move my heart from anxious desperation to expectant waiting for you. Help me to trust in your forgiveness, rest confidently in your faithful love, and wait with hope for your merciful redemption.

The Lord swore to David a sure oath from which he will not turn back:
"One of the sons of your body I will set on your throne."
PSALM 132:11

God's Faithfulness to David

PSALM 132

1*O Lord, remember in David's favor*
all the hardships he endured;
2*how he swore to the Lord*
and vowed to the Mighty One of Jacob,
3*"I will not enter my house*
or get into my bed;
4*I will not give sleep to my eyes*
or slumber to my eyelids,
5*until I find a place for the Lord,*
a dwelling place for the Mighty One of Jacob."

6*We heard of it in Ephrathah;*
we found it in the fields of Jaar.
7*"Let us go to his dwelling place;*
let us worship at his footstool."

8*Rise up, O Lord, and go to your resting place,*
you and the ark of your might.
9*Let your priests be clothed with righteousness,*
and let your faithful shout for joy.

10 *For your servant David's sake*
do not turn away the face of your anointed one.

11 *The Lord swore to David a sure oath*
from which he will not turn back:
"One of the sons of your body
I will set on your throne.
12 *If your sons keep my covenant*
and my decrees that I shall teach them,
their sons also, forevermore,
shall sit on your throne."

13 *For the Lord has chosen Zion;*
he has desired it for his habitation:
14 *"This is my resting place forever;*
here I will reside, for I have desired it.
15 *I will abundantly bless its provisions;*
I will satisfy its poor with bread.
16 *Its priests I will clothe with salvation,*
and its faithful will shout for joy.
17 *There I will cause a horn to sprout up for David;*
I have prepared a lamp for my anointed one.
18 *His enemies I will clothe with disgrace,*
but on him, his crown will gleam."

This royal psalm is composed in two parts: a prayer that the Lord remain faithful to his covenant promises to David and his descendants (verses 1–10) and God's answer to this prayer, reaffirming his everlasting commitment to David and to Zion (verses 11–18). The psalm poetically expresses the events narrated in 2 Samuel 6—7, when David brings the ark of the covenant into Jerusalem and God then promises David an everlasting dynasty. The psalm may have been composed for a liturgical remembrance of these events.

The opening verses flash back to David's time, asking God to remember David's tireless commitment to finding "a dwelling place" for the Lord in which God may be present to his people and worshipped by them (verses 1–5). He vowed not to sleep until he rescued the ark of the covenant from its obscurity and then brought it in procession to Jerusalem (verses 6–9). "Ephrathah" refers to the region around Bethlehem, the hometown of David where his search began, and "the fields of Jaar" is the location where the ark was discovered and from where David brought it up to the holy city. There in Jerusalem God is enthroned over his people with the ark as his "footstool." The sacred ark is borne by priests in festive vestments, accompanied by the joyful shouts of God's people welcoming the Lord to his "resting place" in Zion.

God's response to this prayer is a proclamation of confident hope. God has sworn that one of the descendants of David will forevermore sit on his throne (verses 11–12) and that God will forever rest in Zion, the city of David (verse 13–14). God's eternal dwelling in Zion makes possible the eternity of David's dynasty. God promises a "horn" for David and a "lamp" for his anointed one (verse 17), representing divine power and divine presence in God's chosen king. While the enemies of God's anointed will be disgraced, his gleaming crown will reflect the glory of God (verse 18).

The two halves of the psalm—the voice of prayer and the proclamation of hope—are woven together with key words and phrases. David's devotion to the Lord is matched, and truly is far exceeded, by God's covenant faithfulness to David and his descendant. Corresponding to David's sworn oath (verses 2–5), God swears an oath of his own: the covenant promises concerning the royal line of David (verses 11–12). The conditional nature of the divine promises to David—"If your sons keep my covenant and my decrees that I shall teach them"—serves as an exhortation to David's descendants to follow their forebear's example of faithfulness. And David's procession of the ark to Jerusalem (verses 6–9) is paralleled by the Lord's choice of Zion as his resting place forever (verses 13–16).

Jerusalem and its anointed king, Zion and its Messiah, are indissolubly connected. Place and person together are the manifestation of the kingdom of God. The Lord will not turn back from his oath to David (verse 11) because the Lord has chosen Zion as the place of his dwelling (verse 13). As God's people continued to pray this psalm after the Exile, when they had lost their king and the ark of the covenant, and when their temple was only a shadow of its former glory, the psalm continued to express their hopes for the future. In the Messiah, the lineage of David flowered and came to its fulfillment in the city of Jerusalem. In Jesus Christ and in the new Jerusalem, the reign of God has no end.

Reflection and discussion

- What did David vow to the Lord, and what did the Lord vow to David? How does this psalm encourage fidelity to promises?

- What is the relationship between David and the well-being of God's people?

- What promises in the psalm give Israel hope for its anticipated Messiah?

Prayer

Lord God of Israel, as David swore to find a resting place for you, you assured an eternal dynasty to David. Help me to be faithful to the promises I have made and to be confident in the promises you have made to me.

**O house of Israel, bless the Lord! O house of Aaron, bless the Lord!
O house of Levi, bless the Lord! You that fear the Lord, bless the Lord!**

PSALM 135:19–20

Praise to the Lord of Nature and History

PSALM 135

1*Praise the Lord!*
Praise the name of the Lord;
give praise, O servants of the Lord,
2*you that stand in the house of the Lord,*
in the courts of the house of our God.
3*Praise the Lord, for the Lord is good;*
sing to his name, for he is gracious.
4*For the Lord has chosen Jacob for himself,*
Israel as his own possession.

5*For I know that the Lord is great;*
our Lord is above all gods.
6*Whatever the Lord pleases he does,*
in heaven and on earth,
in the seas and all deeps.
7*He it is who makes the clouds rise at the end of the earth;*
he makes lightnings for the rain
and brings out the wind from his storehouses.

8*He it was who struck down the firstborn of Egypt,*
both human beings and animals;

9 *he sent signs and wonders*
into your midst, O Egypt,
against Pharaoh and all his servants.
10 *He struck down many nations*
and killed mighty kings—
11 *Sihon, king of the Amorites,*
and Og, king of Bashan,
and all the kingdoms of Canaan—
12 *and gave their land as a heritage,*
a heritage to his people Israel.

13 *Your name, O Lord, endures forever,*
your renown, O Lord, throughout all ages.
14 *For the Lord will vindicate his people,*
and have compassion on his servants.

15 *The idols of the nations are silver and gold,*
the work of human hands.
16 *They have mouths, but they do not speak;*
they have eyes, but they do not see;
17 *they have ears, but they do not hear,*
and there is no breath in their mouths.
18 *Those who make them*
and all who trust them
shall become like them.

19 *O house of Israel, bless the Lord!*
O house of Aaron, bless the Lord!
20 *O house of Levi, bless the Lord!*
You that fear the Lord, bless the Lord!
21 *Blessed be the Lord from Zion,*
he who resides in Jerusalem.
Praise the Lord!

Opening and closing with the imperative "Praise the Lord!" this hymn of praise is filled with expressions of acclaim for God. All "servants of the Lord," both the priests who stand in the temple and the laity in the courts of the temple, are summoned to "praise the name of the Lord" and "sing to his name" (verses 1–3). Two motifs appear in these opening lines that will be expanded throughout the psalm: the first is the goodness and graciousness of God, shown in his choosing Israel "as his own possession," and the second is the Lord's greatness, shown in his superiority "above all gods" (verses 4–5).

Because the Lord is both great and gracious, above all gods yet preferential to his own people, he is the master of the natural world as well as master of history. The Lord is totally free and does whatever he wills on the earth, in the seas, and in the heavens (verses 5–7). The clouds, lightning, and wind are simply elements of creation that the Lord commands. At the same time, the Lord has liberated his own people from their bondage in Egypt and struck down many nations to establish the heritage of his people Israel (verses 8–12).

The two motifs appear again as the psalm summarizes what God has done for Israel and contrasts it with what the gods of the nations cannot do. First, the Lord is praised for both the vindication and the compassion he has shown and will continue to demonstrate for his own possession (verses 13–14). Second, the gods of the nations are mere idols, "the work of human hands" (verses 15–17). They look like human beings, but they cannot speak, see, hear, or even breathe. Together, the two motifs serve one point: the contrast between the Lord and his people and the nations and their bogus gods. The Lord made the peoples of the earth in his own image (Gen 1:27), but the nations make their gods in their own image, with mouths, eyes, and ears. All those who make idols and trust in them for their success "shall become like them," lifeless and powerless (verse 18).

The psalm concludes with a call to all in the Israelite community to "bless the Lord!" which expands into a universal call to all who would look upon God with respectful fear (verses 19–20). It moves us from events of biblical history to God's saving presence in our world today. We look back upon the history of our family, our church, and our individual experiences to see countless reasons to "bless the Lord!" The idols of our lives that grasp our attention, like power, pleasure, and privilege, are likewise ineffective and fleeting. Unless we acknowledge that God is the source of our every blessing and the giver of all true gifts, we will turn God's blessings into idols and God's gifts into short-lived possessions. So, after recalling and articulating the history of God's blessings upon us, we rightly return blessings and thankful praise to the Lord.

Reflection and discussion

- Do I pray as God's servant or as if God were my servant? How do the psalms help me become God's servant?

- What are the main differences between the Lord and the gods of other nations?

- In what ways are ancient and modern-day idols the same? In what ways do they differ?

Prayer

Saving Lord, who controls the cosmos and moves the events of history, I praise you for your greatness and your graciousness. May I acknowledge you always as the source of all that I have and all that I am.

SUGGESTIONS FOR FACILITATORS, GROUP SESSION 5

1. Welcome group members and ask if anyone has any questions, announcements, or requests.

2. You may want to pray this prayer as a group:
Ever-living God, who controls the cosmos and moves the events of history, when we cry out to you, come to our aid and hear our prayer. Teach us to avoid greed and restless anxiety, so that we may rest in your faithful love, trust in your forgiveness, and await your merciful redemption. Help us to be confident in the promises you have made to us and faithful to the promises we have made to you. As we seek to live according to your loving plan, may the joy of your peace abide in our hearts and radiate to our families and friends.

3. Ask one or both of the following questions:
   - What most intrigued you from this week's study?
   - What makes you want to know and understand more of God's word?

4. Discuss lessons 19 through 24. Choose one or more of the questions for reflection and discussion from each lesson to talk over as a group.

5. Ask the group members to name one thing they have most appreciated about the way the group has worked during this Bible study. Ask group members to discuss any changes they might suggest in the way the group works in future studies.

6. Invite group members to complete lessons 25 through 30 on their own during the six days before the next meeting. They should write out their own answers to the questions as preparation for next week's session.

7. Ask group members to name ways that their study of these Psalms is enriching their practice of prayer.

8. Conclude by praying aloud together the prayer at the end of one of the lessons discussed. You may want to conclude the prayer by asking members to voice prayers of thanksgiving.

**It is he who remembered us in our low estate,
for his steadfast love endures forever; and rescued us from our foes,
for his steadfast love endures forever.** PSALM 136:23–24

A Litany of God's Faithful Love

PSALM 136

1 *O give thanks to the Lord, for he is good,*
for his steadfast love endures forever.
2 *O give thanks to the God of gods,*
for his steadfast love endures forever.
3 *O give thanks to the Lord of lords,*
for his steadfast love endures forever;

4 *who alone does great wonders,*
for his steadfast love endures forever;
5 *who by understanding made the heavens,*
for his steadfast love endures forever;
6 *who spread out the earth on the waters,*
for his steadfast love endures forever;
7 *who made the great lights,*
for his steadfast love endures forever;
8 *the sun to rule over the day,*
for his steadfast love endures forever;
9 *the moon and stars to rule over the night,*
for his steadfast love endures forever;

10 *who struck Egypt through their firstborn,*

for his steadfast love endures forever;
11 *and brought Israel out from among them,*
for his steadfast love endures forever;
12 *with a strong hand and an outstretched arm,*
for his steadfast love endures forever;
13 *who divided the Red Sea in two,*
for his steadfast love endures forever;
14 *and made Israel pass through the midst of it,*
for his steadfast love endures forever;
15 *but overthrew Pharaoh and his army in the Red Sea,*
for his steadfast love endures forever;
16 *who led his people through the wilderness,*
for his steadfast love endures forever;
17 *who struck down great kings,*
for his steadfast love endures forever;
18 *and killed famous kings,*
for his steadfast love endures forever;
19 *Sihon, king of the Amorites,*
for his steadfast love endures forever;
20 *and Og, king of Bashan,*
for his steadfast love endures forever;
21 *and gave their land as a heritage,*
for his steadfast love endures forever;
22 *a heritage to his servant Israel,*
for his steadfast love endures forever.

23 *It is he who remembered us in our low estate,*
for his steadfast love endures forever;
24 *and rescued us from our foes,*
for his steadfast love endures forever;
25 *who gives food to all flesh,*
for his steadfast love endures forever.

26 *O give thanks to the God of heaven,*
for his steadfast love endures forever.

Imagine a cantor chanting, verse by verse, this prayerful litany, and the congregation responding again and again with the rolling reply: "for his steadfast love endures forever." Or imagine antiphonal choirs, one singing the first line of each verse and another singing the second line. The psalm opens and closes with the call to "give thanks" to the "God of gods" and "the Lord of lords" (verses 1–3). Thanksgiving is the appropriate response for all these blessings bestowed by God on his people because all these divine deeds are marvels far beyond human capacity.

The divine motive for the Lord's blessings in every instance is God's "steadfast love" (in Hebrew, *hesed*). The word expresses what is most distinctive about God's love revealed in the covenant with Israel. It is a passionate, divine care, a love that is faithful, loyal, and steadfast. This publicly performed psalm is a way of remembering and celebrating God's enduring love, a collective expression that keeps alive the many experiences of God's saving deeds throughout history.

Following the invitation to express thanks to the Lord, the psalm focuses on creation as tangible evidence of God's steadfast love (verses 4–9). God's love is shown by the fact that he made the skies, that he fixed the earth firmly in its place amid the subterranean waters, that he made the "great lights" of sun and moon and stars. For all these deeds of constant love he is deserving of thanks.

Yet, God not only established the cosmos but entered into Israel's history in an astonishing fashion. Through the events of the exodus, God liberated his own "with a strong hand and an outstretched arm" (verses 10–15). The litany continues with those events that assured Israel of settling in the land of promise and building a heritage there (verses 16–22). Each verse presents a new episode in the saga of God's way with Israel, but the refrain chants what is always the same. The divine love manifested in the covenant continues age after age.

The use of the word "us" in the concluding verses refers to God's blessings for the current generation (verses 23–24). For all who chant this psalm, God's saving works continue in the present moment and will continue unwaveringly into the future. God's "steadfast love" has been active since the beginning of creation and continues today. It extends even to the nourishment of every creature (verse 25). This faithful love of "the God of heaven" touches all reality and transcends everything.

Reflection and discussion

- Why do the psalms encourage us to give continual thanks for all the "great wonders" that God has done for us?

- What does this psalm indicate about the value of repetitive prayer?

- What three new verses would I add to this litany to indicate how God has guided and directed my own life?

Prayer

God of gods and Lord of lords, we thank you for the great wonders you show to us from age to age. We trust that your steadfast love will fill our lives in the present moment and continue unwaveringly into the future.

Though I walk in the midst of trouble, you preserve me against the wrath of my enemies; you stretch out your hand, and your right hand delivers me. PSALM 138:7

Remembering Both Blessings and Adversities

PSALM 137

1 *By the rivers of Babylon—*
there we sat down and there we wept
when we remembered Zion.
2 *On the willows there*
we hung up our harps.
3 *For there our captors*
asked us for songs,
and our tormentors asked for mirth, saying,
"Sing us one of the songs of Zion!"

4 *How could we sing the Lord's song*
in a foreign land?
5 *If I forget you, O Jerusalem,*
let my right hand wither!
6 *Let my tongue cling to the roof of my mouth,*
if I do not remember you,
if I do not set Jerusalem
above my highest joy.

7 *Remember, O Lord, against the Edomites*
the day of Jerusalem's fall,
how they said, "Tear it down! Tear it down!

Down to its foundations!"
8*O daughter Babylon, you devastator!*
Happy shall they be who pay you back
what you have done to us!
9*Happy shall they be who take your little ones*
and dash them against the rock!

PSALM 138

1*I give you thanks, O Lord, with my whole heart;*
before the gods I sing your praise;
2*I bow down toward your holy temple*
and give thanks to your name for your steadfast love and your faithfulness;
for you have exalted your name and your word
above everything.
3*On the day I called, you answered me,*
you increased my strength of soul.
4*All the kings of the earth shall praise you, O Lord,*
for they have heard the words of your mouth.
5*They shall sing of the ways of the Lord,*
for great is the glory of the Lord.
6*For though the Lord is high, he regards the lowly;*
but the haughty he perceives from far away.

7*Though I walk in the midst of trouble,*
you preserve me against the wrath of my enemies;
you stretch out your hand,
and your right hand delivers me.
8*The Lord will fulfill his purpose for me;*
your steadfast love, O Lord, endures forever.
Do not forsake the work of your hands.

The psalmist of Psalm 137 must have been one of the temple musicians taken into exile with harp and sacred music. Captive in Babylon, these citizens of Zion fondly remember their city and weep for its loss. The cruelty of deportation haunts their memory: they lost their temple, where God was present for them; their king, through whom God extended his rule; and their land, through which God blessed their heritage. The recollection of such a loss evokes the powerful emotions expressed in the psalm: melancholy, nostalgia, heartache, and passionate rage.

The psalmist and his guild of musicians were the targets of their captors' cruel humor. Though they had hung up their harps in mourning, their captors taunted them with sarcastic jibes: "Sing us one of the songs of Zion!" (137:2–3). But their trauma is too deep; this was the very Zion that Babylon destroyed. Singing the joyful songs of Zion in that foreign land would be an insult to the memory of their beloved city. So, they vow to remember their city, uttering a kind of self-curse should they ever forget. "Let my right hand wither!"—the hand that plucks the harp; "Let my tongue cling to the roof of my mouth"—the tongue that sings the sacred songs (137:5–6).

As the musicians remember Jerusalem, their passion boils up and spills over into bitter scorn (137:7–9). The Edomites had allied with the Babylonians and torn the city down to its foundations. They pray that those who dishonored their noble city get what they deserve. After invoking "daughter Babylon," they begin with the traditional beatitude, "Happy shall they be," and then turn it into a violent malediction. The final curse, expressing the horrid wish to slaughter young children, can be understood as the desire to deny the Babylonians a future. It is an expression of rage on the lips of powerless victims, not a program of action.

While we remember that the psalm is poetry, not ethical instruction, we must also keep in mind that it is a prayer. As such, the cry of rage is lifted not in an angry fist against a human enemy but in prayer to the God who claims the sole right to execute vengeance. To pray such a psalm is to release the rage to God, to let God absorb the violence, and to ask that our enemies be driven into the hands of God.

Babylon is both Israel's historical enemy and the symbolic expression of the evil that constantly assaults God's plans for his people. In the books of Daniel and Revelation, Babylon represents all the worldly powers in opposition to the city of God. While Psalm 137 expresses rage against enemies, Psalm 138 expresses confidence in God's protection against the enemies' wrath. Again and again, the psalmists agonize over those who are opposed to them; those who threaten them, both with speech and with swords; those who plot against them; those who make them the object of their mockery; those who would be glad to see them in their grave; etc., etc. Moreover, the psalmist actively wants their destruction, their defeat, their humiliation.

This preoccupation with enemies arises from a realistic perspective. The simple truth is that, in a fallen world, those who are righteous will have enemies, and the more righteous they are, the more of them they will have. The person with no enemies, as Churchill rightly saw, is not to be trusted, for he stands for nothing.

There is, of course, no better example of this principle than Jesus himself in relation to his contemporaries. As the gospels unfold, we see the army of Jesus' antagonists increasing exponentially, and by the end of the narrative, those opponents put him to death. So intense is the opposition to him that we can speak of the sins of the world being placed upon him. To be sure, Jesus consistently urged the love of one's enemies and, from the cross, he uttered a word of forgiveness to those who were putting him to death. But in order to love our enemies, we have to have some enemies.

We can read the "enemies" and "foes" of the psalms as symbols of the evil powers that constantly assault God's plan for his people. We can trust that when we "walk in the midst of trouble," God will preserve us against the wrath of our enemies and deliver us from their grasp (138:7). For we know that "the Lord will fulfill his purpose for me," and we can offer grateful praise to God: "Your steadfast love, O Lord, endures forever" (138:8).

Reflection and discussion

- Why is the taunting demand of the Babylonian captors—that the musicians sing songs of Zion—so offensive?

- Is it acceptable to express rage to God in prayer? What do I do with the fury and wrath that lies in my memory?

Prayer

Lord God, help me remember the blessings of the past so that I may give you thanks, and help me remember the hardships of the past so that I can learn and grow stronger. Your steadfast love endures forever.

Search me, O God, and know my heart; test me and know my thoughts. See if there is any wicked way in me, and lead me in the way everlasting. PSALM 139:23–24

God Searches Me and Knows My Heart

PSALM 139

1*O Lord, you have searched me and known me.*
2*You know when I sit down and when I rise up;*
you discern my thoughts from far away.
3*You search out my path and my lying down,*
and are acquainted with all my ways.
4*Even before a word is on my tongue,*
O Lord, you know it completely.
5*You hem me in, behind and before,*
and lay your hand upon me.
6*Such knowledge is too wonderful for me;*
it is so high that I cannot attain it.

7*Where can I go from your spirit?*
Or where can I flee from your presence?
8*If I ascend to heaven, you are there;*
if I make my bed in Sheol, you are there.
9*If I take the wings of the morning*
and settle at the farthest limits of the sea,
10*even there your hand shall lead me,*
and your right hand shall hold me fast.

11*If I say, "Surely the darkness shall cover me,*
and the light around me become night,"
12*even the darkness is not dark to you;*
the night is as bright as the day,
for darkness is as light to you.

13*For it was you who formed my inward parts;*
you knit me together in my mother's womb.
14*I praise you, for I am fearfully and wonderfully made.*
Wonderful are your works;
that I know very well.
15*My frame was not hidden from you,*
when I was being made in secret,
intricately woven in the depths of the earth.
16*Your eyes beheld my unformed substance.*
In your book were written
all the days that were formed for me,
when none of them as yet existed.
17*How weighty to me are your thoughts, O God!*
How vast is the sum of them!
18*I try to count them—they are more than the sand;*
I come to the end—I am still with you.

19*O that you would kill the wicked, O God,*
and that the bloodthirsty would depart from me—
20*those who speak of you maliciously,*
and lift themselves up against you for evil!
21*Do I not hate those who hate you, O Lord?*
And do I not loathe those who rise up against you?
22*I hate them with perfect hatred;*
I count them my enemies.
23*Search me, O God, and know my heart;*
test me and know my thoughts.
24*See if there is any wicked way in me,*
and lead me in the way everlasting.

This most intimate of psalms defies categorization. Is it a song of praise, a prayer of contrition, an individual lament, or a wisdom psalm? While the psalm contains elements of each of these forms, no one of them fully accounts for the content and structure of the psalm. It contains several allusions to the book of Job, evoking the image of a righteous sufferer who seeks to be tried by God and found innocent. The psalm ends as it begins, with a plea for God to "search" me, to "know" me, and to "test" me (verses 1, 23). Finally, the psalmist longs to be found righteous in God's sight: to "see" if there is any wicked way in me and "lead" me in the way everlasting (verse 24).

The four stanzas of this psalm speak to the intimate relationship between the one praying and God. The Lord knows the psalmist completely (verses 1–6), is present where the psalmist is (verses 7–12), and was fashioning the psalmist's being even before his birth (verses 13–18). Even the final section, which reveals the psalmist's hatred for the wicked, is a Hebrew way of speaking about the psalmist's closeness to God and distance from evildoers (verses 19–24). In all of its parts, the psalm expresses the psalmist's existence as totally within the knowledge, work, and ways of the Lord.

This psalm is often described as a meditation on God's omniscience in the first stanza, God omnipresence in the second stanza, and God's omnipotence in the third stanza, but God nevertheless displays a striking interest in the individual person expressing this prayer. Although God knows all things, is present everywhere, and is all-powerful, the individual is enclosed in the divine reality. The Lord knows whatever the psalmist does or thinks; the Lord is present to the psalmist wherever he is; and the Lord formed the psalmist from the first moment of his existence. Even at the end of life, he will be able to say, "I am still with you" (verse 18).

The psalm is characterized by the use of opposites: "when I sit down" and "when I rise up" (verse 2); "my path" and "my lying down" (verse 3); "behind and before" (verse 5); "to heaven" and "in Sheol" (verse 8); the east, "the wings of the morning," and the west, "the farthest limits of the sea" (verse 9); "the darkness" and "the light" (verse 11); "night" and "day" (verse 12). God encompasses all space and time, yet is intimately close; he is within and without, from beginning to end. Though God does not move from place to place as we do, yet God is present in every place. He is totally present, and no one can escape the divine reach.

For all who make this prayer their own, this understanding of God can evoke fear and wonder. Such scrutiny of our lives can cause us to withdraw, or it can inspire us with trusting confidence. Yet, as the psalmist experienced, even when we flee from God, his hand will hold us fast and lead us "in the way everlasting." As we reflect on our relationship with God through this ancient psalm, we deepen our desire for God's presence and his way. And we surrender our lives to God's pursuit and rest in his all-knowing presence and his everlasting love.

Reflection and discussion

- In what ways is the psalm an argument for engaging in a relationship with God?

- When I consider the closeness of my relationship with God, who knew me even before I was born, what feelings arise within me at the thought of such familiarity with God?

- In what ways does God's knowledge and love of me lead me to want to know and love others?

Prayer

You search me, O God, and you know my heart. You understand me more than I understand myself, and you care about every aspect of my existence. Guide the path of my life and lead me in the way everlasting.

Bring me out of prison, so that I may give thanks to your name.
The righteous will surround me, for you will deal bountifully with me.
PSALM 142:7

Prayers for Those Who Are Alone and Threatened

PSALM 141

1 *I call upon you, O Lord; come quickly to me;*
give ear to my voice when I call to you.
2 *Let my prayer be counted as incense before you,*
and the lifting up of my hands as an evening sacrifice.

3 *Set a guard over my mouth, O Lord;*
keep watch over the door of my lips.
4 *Do not turn my heart to any evil,*
to busy myself with wicked deeds
in company with those who work iniquity;
do not let me eat of their delicacies.

5 *Let the righteous strike me;*
let the faithful correct me.
Never let the oil of the wicked anoint my head,
for my prayer is continually against their wicked deeds.
6 *When they are given over to those who shall condemn them,*
then they shall learn that my words were pleasant.
7 *Like a rock that one breaks apart and shatters on the land,*
so shall their bones be strewn at the mouth of Sheol.

8 But my eyes are turned toward you, O God, my Lord;
in you I seek refuge; do not leave me defenseless.
9 Keep me from the trap that they have laid for me,
and from the snares of evildoers.
10 Let the wicked fall into their own nets,
while I alone escape.

PSALM 142

1 With my voice I cry to the Lord;
with my voice I make supplication to the Lord.
2 I pour out my complaint before him;
I tell my trouble before him.
3 When my spirit is faint,
you know my way.

In the path where I walk
they have hidden a trap for me.
4 Look on my right hand and see—
there is no one who takes notice of me;
no refuge remains to me;
no one cares for me.

5 I cry to you, O Lord;
I say, "You are my refuge,
my portion in the land of the living."
6 Give heed to my cry,
for I am brought very low.

Save me from my persecutors,
for they are too strong for me.
7 Bring me out of prison,
so that I may give thanks to your name.
The righteous will surround me,
for you will deal bountifully with me.

Throughout the history of Christian worship, Psalm 141 has been the preeminent psalm for the church's evening prayer. It presents the image of prayer rising to God like the ascending incense and hands lifted in prayer like an evening sacrifice offered to God on the altar (141:2). We can imagine these words being chanted in the temple of Jerusalem during the offering of incense as the high priest lit the lamps each evening. The images of incense and sacrifice turn the thoughts of Christians to Jesus, who "gave himself up for us, a fragrant offering and sacrifice to God" (Eph 5:2).

The evening sacrifice at the temple prepared for the true oblation offered when the Lamb of God, nailed to the cross, lifted his hands to the Father in his perfect self-offering for the salvation of the world. Whenever, then, we raise our hands in prayer, as Paul tells us to do (1 Tim 2:8), we signify that our relationship to God is founded on the power of the cross. The lifting of our hands in prayer is acceptable to God because of its relationship to Christ's perfect sacrifice, through which we draw near to God.

The significance of the rising smoke of incense is most clearly expressed in John's vision of the heavenly throne room. The angel stood at the altar with a golden censer, "and the smoke of the incense, with the prayers of the saints, rose before God from the hand of the angel" (Rev 8:3–4). As the church offers its evening prayer, it is lifted to heaven to adore the Lamb together with the angels and saints. As a result, the daily evening prayer joins the church both to the heavenly throne room of the Lamb and the hill of Golgotha on which he took away the sins of the world.

The psalmist is clearly in distress, calling upon the Lord to restrain him from temptations and to protect him from the schemes of evildoers (141:3–4). He knows that he must keep his distance from the wicked, recognizing that it is better to receive a striking rebuke from a righteous person than to be praised and anointed with oil by a wicked one (141:5). Finally, the psalmist prays that God defend him from the traps and snares of evildoers (141:8–10). Rather, he asks, "Let the wicked fall into their own nets," ensnared in their own devices.

In Psalm 142, the psalmist describes his prayerful plea to the Lord: "I pour out my complaint before him" (142:1–2). He honestly speaks about his troubles in God's presence. And because these prayerful complaints are not specified, they may express the varied experiences of anyone who wishes to cry out to the Lord.

Trustingly, the psalmist cries, "You know my way" (142:3). God's knowing his way is vital because in this path, his persecutors "have hidden a trap." The psalmist confesses feeling profoundly alone and helpless: "There is no one who takes notice of me; no refuge remains to me; no one cares for me" (142:4). Again, the poet expresses a universal sentiment: struggling between the feeling of trust in God and the emotions of lonesomeness.

The psalmist trustingly knows that God is his "refuge," yet he admits that he is "brought very low" and pleads for God's help (142:4–5). His reference to confinement—"Bring me out of prison"—is ambiguous, perhaps intentionally so (142:7). It may refer to physical custody or it may be a metaphor for the captivity he feels in distress. Certainly, this opacity renders the psalm open to be chanted by anyone who is bound and shut up in all sorts of ways.

Both of these psalms move from the psalmist's distress to confidence in God's saving presence. God provides escape from the traps and snares of the evildoers, and God moves the poet from prison to praise. The psalmist concludes his prayer with confidence that God "will deal bountifully" and that he will be reincorporated into the community of believers.

Reflection and discussion

- How free do I feel to cry out to the Lord with supplication and complaint?

- In what prisons or snares do I feel captive? How do I experience God's liberating power?

Prayer

Lord God, you are my refuge. Protect me from the snares that threaten me along the path of life, and release me from the prison that holds me bound. Give me confidence that I am supported by a community of believers and your abundant care.

I will sing a new song to you, O God; upon a ten-stringed harp I will play to you, the one who gives victory to kings, who rescues his servant David. PSALM 144:9–10

Happy the People Whose God Is the Lord

PSALM 144

1 *Blessed be the Lord, my rock,*
who trains my hands for war, and my fingers for battle;
2 *my rock and my fortress,*
my stronghold and my deliverer,
my shield, in whom I take refuge,
who subdues the peoples under me.

3 *O Lord, what are human beings that you regard them,*
or mortals that you think of them?
4 *They are like a breath;*
their days are like a passing shadow.

5 *Bow your heavens, O Lord, and come down;*
touch the mountains so that they smoke.
6 *Make the lightning flash and scatter them;*
send out your arrows and rout them.
7 *Stretch out your hand from on high;*
set me free and rescue me from the mighty waters,
from the hand of aliens,
8 *whose mouths speak lies,*
and whose right hands are false.

9I will sing a new song to you, O God;
upon a ten-stringed harp I will play to you,
10the one who gives victory to kings,
who rescues his servant David.
11Rescue me from the cruel sword,
and deliver me from the hand of aliens,
whose mouths speak lies,
and whose right hands are false.

12May our sons in their youth
be like plants full grown,
our daughters like corner pillars,
cut for the building of a palace.
13May our barns be filled,
with produce of every kind;
may our sheep increase by thousands,
by tens of thousands in our fields,
14and may our cattle be heavy with young.
May there be no breach in the walls, no exile,
and no cry of distress in our streets.

15Happy are the people to whom such blessings fall;
happy are the people whose God is the Lord.

The implied speaker of this psalm is the king from the lineage of David who sits on the throne of Judah. The king knows that the Lord is still the protector of God's people as he was during the reign of David, and he urges God to intervene in the present threat to deliver God's people from their foes.

The king offers words of praise and blessing to God, who is "my rock," "my fortress," "my stronghold," "my deliverer," and "my shield," the one who shelters the king and deflects the flaming arrows of the enemy (verses 1–2). Such descriptions would imply that the Lord is the one who takes action while the king remains passive. But the king acknowledges that the Lord is his tutor in the art of combat, the one who "trains my hand for war, and my fingers for battle." In comparison with so great a Lord, any human being, even a king, seems as short-lived as "a breath," "like a passing shadow," unworthy to be the recipient of such help from God (verses 3–4).

Those who continue to pray this psalm through the ages may reinterpret the militaristic language in the way that Paul suggests. He urges Christians to be strong in the Lord for the spiritual battles they face: "Put on the whole armor of God, so that you may be able to stand against the wiles of the devil. For our struggle is not against enemies of blood and flesh, but against the rulers, against the authorities, against the cosmic powers of this present darkness, against the spiritual forces of evil in the heavenly places" (Eph 6:11–12).

Then, suddenly, the king is pleading for the Lord's intervention (verses 5–8), saying, "Bow your heavens, O Lord" and asking God to come down to earth and act. The language recalls the Lord's appearance at Sinai, when the mountain smoked as a result of God's coming near. The lightning bolts are God's arrows, scattering the enemies and rescuing God's people from the tumultuous waters, representing the political powers asserting themselves against Israel. The king pleads for God to stretch out his hand, to liberate and save his people from their enemies, who are not only strong in might but deceptive in their speech and false in taking oaths and negotiating treaties.

The psalmist turns again to praising God, this time with a newly composed song accompanied by the harp (verse 9). The Lord is described as "the one who gives victory to kings, who rescues his servant David" (verse 10). The psalmist makes clear that God's action in relationship to David was not unique to him but forms the pattern for God's relating to the kings of David's lineage, and indeed with his heritage through the ages. This declaration leads to the king's further plea, asking for rescue from "the cruel sword" and deliverance from their enemies (verse 11).

The final section of the psalm leaps beyond relief from an immediate crisis to describing the fullness of life that follows the people's deliverance (verse 12–14). It jumps from the individual concerns of the king, told in the first person singular, to those of the nation for whom he struggles, told in the first person plural. The vision of the future looks first to the coming generation, to "our sons in their youth" who are strong like olive trees, to "our daughters like corner pillars," young and shapely like the decorative pillars in a palace. The vision continues with barns filled with produce, fields filled with sheep for milk and wool, and cattle that are heavily pregnant. Finally, the vision describes the city with no breach in its walls and thus no one needing to leave the city to go into exile when it is captured. Then there will be no cry of grief and anguish in the streets. "Happy" indeed is the people who have proven what it is like to have the Lord as their God (verse 15).

Reflection and discussion

- How might it be helpful to reflect on the brevity of life?

- When do I feel most confident before God? When do I feel least confident before God?

- If the psalmist seems unduly concerned with the material blessings hoped for from God, how does the final line express the blessing to be prized above all others?

Prayer

O God, my stronghold and deliverer, be my refuge and shield against the forces that wage war against me. Protect me against those seeking to destroy your rule over my heart. Bless me with your abundance and peace.

Your kingdom is an everlasting kingdom, and your dominion endures throughout all generations. The Lord is faithful in all his words, and gracious in all his deeds. PSALM 145:13

The Kingdom of Our Royal Lord

PSALM 145

1 *I will extol you, my God and King,*
and bless your name forever and ever.
2 *Every day I will bless you,*
and praise your name forever and ever.
3 *Great is the Lord, and greatly to be praised;*
his greatness is unsearchable.

4 *One generation shall laud your works to another,*
and shall declare your mighty acts.
5 *On the glorious splendor of your majesty,*
and on your wondrous works, I will meditate.
6 *The might of your awesome deeds shall be proclaimed,*
and I will declare your greatness.
7 *They shall celebrate the fame of your abundant goodness,*
and shall sing aloud of your righteousness.

8 *The Lord is gracious and merciful,*
slow to anger and abounding in steadfast love.
9 *The Lord is good to all,*
and his compassion is over all that he has made.

10 *All your works shall give thanks to you, O Lord,*
and all your faithful shall bless you.
11 *They shall speak of the glory of your kingdom,*
and tell of your power,
12 *to make known to all people your mighty deeds,*
and the glorious splendor of your kingdom.
13 *Your kingdom is an everlasting kingdom,*
and your dominion endures throughout all generations.

The Lord is faithful in all his words,
and gracious in all his deeds.
14 *The Lord upholds all who are falling,*
and raises up all who are bowed down.
15 *The eyes of all look to you,*
and you give them their food in due season.
16 *You open your hand,*
satisfying the desire of every living thing.
17 *The Lord is just in all his ways,*
and kind in all his doings.
18 *The Lord is near to all who call on him,*
to all who call on him in truth.
19 *He fulfills the desire of all who fear him;*
he also hears their cry, and saves them.
20 *The Lord watches over all who love him,*
but all the wicked he will destroy.

21 *My mouth will speak the praise of the Lord,*
and all flesh will bless his holy name forever and ever.

Psalm 145 appears in Jewish prayer books more than any other psalm. The great Psalm scroll from Qumran contains a version of the psalm in which the refrain "Blessed is the Lord and blessed is his name forever and ever" is included after each verse. And the Talmud, the primary text for Rabbinic Judaism, urges that Psalm 145, like the Shema, be recited three times a day. All indications conclude that the words of this psalm were and are a vital part of the faith of the Jewish people. The high regard of this psalm in both the synagogue and the church is based on the comprehensive range of its praise and thanksgiving to God.

The psalm is an acrostic poem, in which the Hebrew text contains twenty-one lines, each beginning with the next letter of the alphabet. It begins with a proclamation of praise and blessing for "my God and King" (verses 1–2). The psalm's intricate structure alternates between "you" sections, addressing the Lord directly, and "he" sections, referring to the Lord in the third person. Generally, the "you" sections describe the act of praising God (verses 1–2, 4–7), and the "he" sections describe the qualities of God and the substance of the praise (verses 3, 8–9).

As the psalm progresses, it declares the reasons for praising and blessing the name of God the king. These reasons are many and varied, but they point essentially to God's greatness, goodness, and mercy. The individual singer persuades one generation after another to join in the act of praise for God's mighty acts. So, together, the singer and the generations declare the great and good and merciful acts of God the king.

At the center of the psalm, three consecutive verses begin with the Hebrew letters *kaph, lamed,* and *mem,* the three letters that form the word for "king" (*melek,* in Hebrew). In these verses, the word "kingdom" (formed from the same three-letter root) occurs four times (verses 11–13). These central verses emphasize the theme of the psalm: the kingship of God over all peoples and throughout all generations.

The scope of God's care is inclusive of all. The Lord lifts up all who are falling, gives food to all who look to him, acts justly and kindly in all his ways, and is near to all who call on him (verses 14–17). There is no distinction between Israelites and people of other nations, Jews and Gentiles. The Lord satisfies and saves "all who call on him," "all who fear him," and "all who love him" (verses 18–20). The only exclusion is for those who choose a life of wickedness.

The remarkable lesson of this psalm of praise is this: God's glorious and everlasting kingdom, to which Israel's experience is a testimony, is open to all. The reign of our God and King has no boundaries. "All flesh will bless his holy name forever and ever" (verse 21). This is the message that the New Testament writers will explain and expand.

Reflection and discussion

- How many times does the word "all" appear in the psalm? What does this indicate about the psalm's message?

- Of all the reasons given for praising my God and King, which do I most want to experience forever?

- How have the church's evening psalms helped me to pray better?

Prayer

My Royal Lord, one generation after another praises you for your greatness, goodness, and mercy. May you reign forever over your glorious kingdom, and may I always bless your holy name.

SUGGESTIONS FOR FACILITATORS, GROUP SESSION 6

1. Welcome group members and make any final announcements or requests.

2. You may want to pray this prayer as a group:
   God of gods and Lord of lords, we praise you for your greatness, goodness, and mercy. We thank you for the great wonders you show to us from age to age. Be our stronghold and deliverer, our refuge and shield, against the forces seeking to destroy your rule over our hearts. We trust that your steadfast love will fill our lives in the present moment and continue unwaveringly into the future. Give us confidence that we are supported by a community of believers and blessed with your abundance and peace.

3. Ask one or both of the following questions:
   - How has this study of the psalms enriched your life?
   - In what way has this study challenged you the most?

4. Discuss lessons 25 through 30. Choose one or more of the questions for reflection and discussion from each lesson to discuss as a group.

5. Ask the group if they would like to study another title in the series. Discuss the topic and dates and make a decision among those interested. Ask the group members to suggest people they would like to invite to participate in the next study series.

6. Ask the group to discuss the insights that stand out most from this study over the past six weeks.

7. Conclude by praying aloud the following prayer or another of your own choosing:
   Holy Spirit of the living God, you inspired the writers of the Scriptures and you have guided our study during these weeks. Continue to deepen our love for the word of God in the holy Scriptures and draw us more deeply into a life of prayer. We thank you for the confident hope you have placed within us and for the gifts that build up the church. Through this study, lead us to worship and witness more fully and fervently, and bless us now and always with the fire of your love.